The Ultimate Officer Candidate School Guidebook

What You Need to Know to Succeed at Federal and State OCS

Capt. Ryan Pierce
(Washington Army National Guard)

SB
Savas Beatie
California and New York

Cataloging-in-Publication Data is available from the Library of Congress.

First edition, first printing
10 9 8 7 6 5 4 3 2 1

ISBN-13: 978-1-932714-91-3

SB

Published by
Savas Beatie LLC
521 Fifth Avenue, Suite 1700
New York, NY 10175
Phone: 916-941-6896

Editorial Offices:

Savas Beatie LLC
P.O. Box 4527
El Dorado Hills, CA 95762
Phone: 916-941-6896 / (E-mail) sales@savasbeatie.com

Front Cover: LT Taylor, P.

Photos, pages 100-113: CPT Eric Armstrong

All photos and graphics are courtesy of the author

Proudly printed and bound in the United States of America.

This book is dedicated to my beautiful wife Megan. Her strength, patience, and encouragement are what allow me to continue to serve my country and pursue projects like writing this book. I would also like to dedicate this book to every soldier I've had the opportunity to serve with. Good or bad, you have all made me the officer I am today and I thank you for that.

Please Note:

The fitness program presented in this book was not designed by a licensed physician. You should consult with a physician before beginning any fitness program or exercises discussed in this book. All forms of exercise pose some inherent risk, even for people in top physical condition. The author, and everyone who contributed to this book, advises readers to take full responsibility for their safety and know their limitations. The statements (and illustrations) in this book are the opinion of the author.

Contents

Contents (continued)

Preface

I was 25 years old with a Bachelor's Degree and a good career making a nice living when I made the decision in late 2002 to enter the United States military. Everything I knew about the Army I had learned from my father while tagging along with him during his Army Reserve drill weekends. When I was 11 I thought soldiers were cool. They got to play with really awesome equipment, or what seemed like really awesome equipment to me at that young age. The events of September 11, 2001 shocked me. I spent the next year wondering if I was doing everything I could to support our nation. Once I concluded I was not, I chose to follow in my father's footsteps into the Army. Ever since I can remember my dad spoke to me about joining the service. He would say, 'if you do join, you should go the Officer route." Naturally, when I did enlist, I signed a contract referred to as O9S, or officer enlistment option. This meant I would attend basic training for nine weeks then attend officer candidate school. In my case, as a member of the Washington Army National Guard, upon completion of basic training, I returned to my state and began OCS.

I attended basic training at Fort Knox, Kentucky for nine weeks beginning in March 2003. My drill sergeants assigned me as Platoon Guide day one of "going down range." I don't know if they did this by accident but I worked hard and never relinquished my position. I graduated in June 2003 as Distinguished Honor Graduate. The success I achieved individually gave me confidence moving into officer candidate school, but it did not prepare me for what was in store.

I was told by people who never attended OCS that it was a "gentleman's course." Within my first two days at the Alabama Military Academy at Fort McClellan I knew it was anything but a "gentleman's course." Three phases and nine weeks later, I graduated and was sent back to my state for commissioning in the Washington Army National Guard. Since earning my commission I've been assigned as a platoon leader and an executive officer. For the last three years I've served as a TAC officer for B/CO for 1/205th Training Regiment in Redmond, Washington. I've experienced OCS from two perspectives: a successful candidate and as a successful TAC officer.

This guide is relatively short and easy to read. If you are an ambitious enlisted soldier on active duty or in the reserves looking for an opportunity to become a lieutenant, this book is for you. My target audience included veterans who left the military and used the GI Bill to earn an undergraduate degree and are now considering getting back in, maybe even considering earning a commission. This book includes the information any candidate must need to be successful during OCS.

Again, I cannot stress this enough, if you are considering earning your commission for selfish reasons, please do not read this book and please do not attend OCS because the Army needs altruistic leaders who display all of the Army Values in and out of uniform.

Ryan Pierce

Introduction

In 1939, Gen. George Marshall recognized the importance and necessity of new company grade officers, especially if the U.S. was thrust into the conflict raging in Europe and Asia. In the summer of 1940 his idea of a rigorous officer training facility was put into motion at Fort Benning, Georgia. Infantry, Field Artillery, and Coastal Artillery Officer Candidate Schools were the only three branches trained during the first class; other branches would follow. The first class began with 204 candidates; 171 graduated as second lieutenants on September 27, 1941, under the watchful eye of the school's first commandant, Brig. Gen. Asa L. Singleton. General Singleton was the architect of the modern Officer Candidate School.

More than 100,000 candidates were enrolled in 448 OCS classes between July 1941 and May 1947. The attrition rate was high; about 1 in 3 did not complete the training and earn a commission. OCS classes stopped after WWII except for the Ground General School in Fort Riley, Kansas, where the final class graduated only 52 second lieutenants in November 1947. OCS went away until the need for company grade leaders came about during the winter of 1951.

Shortages of company grade officers during the Korean War reopened OCS in February of 1951, when the 17-week course increased to 22 weeks. In August of 1953, OCS was reduced from eight programs to three: Infantry, Artillery, and Engineer.

Before we became deeply involved in the Vietnam War, OCS was reduced from three branches to two: Infantry and Field Artillery. At the height of the Vietnam War, OCS grew to five programs and produced 7,000 officers per year from the five battalions at Fort

Benning. This era gave birth to the term "90-day wonder," meant to describe the new second lieutenant with very little experience to balance his great responsibility. As the Vietnam War wound down, OCS was again reduced to two programs: Infantry and Female OCS. Female officer candidates were trained at Fort McClellan, Alabama, while Infantry candidates remained at Fort Benning. Infantry OCS was reduced to one battalion and remains this size today.

Branch Immaterial Officer Candidate School began in April of 1973 in order to replace the branch-specific courses and the length of the course was reduced to 14 weeks. Female officer candidates remained at Fort McClellan until December 1976, when their program merged with the branch immaterial OCS program at Fort Benning.

Currently, active component (Federal) OCS is 12 weeks long and is branch immaterial with male and female candidates training together. The Army Reserves typically sends their candidates to the 14-week Federal school at Fort Benning. They are now initiating the process of sending reserve candidates to the Army National Guard traditional OCS program, consisting of a two-week Phase One, 12-month Phase Two spread out over drill weekends, and a two-week consolidated Phase Three. The course management program (CMP) was standardized by Fort Benning in 1998 for all OCS programs. Therefore, the entire training curriculum is exactly the same. The biggest differences between the active duty 12-week OCS program and the National Guard nine-week Fast Track are options and location. Active duty offers OCS in one 12-week chunk and the reserve component (State OCS) offers an 18-month one weekend a month, two-weeks a year schedule, as well as a nine-week fast track option during summer and winter seasons.

What you are about to read will prepare you for all OCS options. Keep an open mind and do not let the complex idea of being a leader take your mind off of your goal, which is to earn your commission as a second lieutenant. OCS is the first step in a long journey. Read this book and you will be prepared.

“Excellence doesn’t happen by accident. It takes preparation, teamwork, consistency, and dedication.”

— Christopher Lewis

Chapter 1

Why do You Want to be an Officer?

"A man who will not protect his freedom does not deserve to be free."

— General Douglas MacArthur

Here is the first thing you need to ask yourself: "Why am I doing this?" If it's for higher pay, please put this book down and reconsider your motivation because you will not make it through Officer Candidate School (OCS). While there is no 100% correct response to this question, there are a few 100% wrong answers. Here are a few wrong answers:

- I like to be in charge.
- Officers don't have to work as hard.
- Officers are less likely to die in combat.
- I want to be called, "Sir or Ma'am."
- I earned a degree and I think I'm pretty smart.

Earning a commission as a Second Lieutenant (2LT) in the United States Army is an honor and a privilege. In this book you will never read "took" or "got" a commission. Why? Because if you successfully complete OCS or any other commissioning source, you will have earned it.

Ways to Earn a Commission in the U.S. Army

United States Military Academy at West Point

West Point is one of the country's top universities. It is a competitive environment that produces some of the nation's best leaders. Many graduates of the Academy at West Point become leaders in the military, in government, and in the civilian world. Examples of West Point graduates include General (and President) Dwight D. Eisenhower and astronaut (and command module pilot of Apollo 11) Buzz Aldrin.

Requirements

If you're up for the challenge, listed below are some of the basic academic requirements for West Point. An applicant must be:

- At least 17 years old and not have reached your 23rd birthday by July 1 of year admitted
- A U.S. citizen
- Single
- Not pregnant or with any legal obligation to support a child or children
- Congressionally nominated or have a service-connected nomination
- A recipient of strong scores on either college entrance exam ACT or SAT
- Have an above-average high school or college academic record

Advantages

I put West Point in the same group as the Ivy League schools. The education is second to none but upon graduation students are commissioned as second lieutenants in the U.S Army and sent to their first assignment: Officer Basic Course. The rest of American college graduates are left to fend for themselves in the civilian work force. A vast majority of generals on active duty and the reserve component are graduates of West Point. Non-academy graduates can and do make the rank of general (Colin Powell, for example), but the majority seem to be West Point graduates.

Disadvantages

Some graduates leave the academy with a huge ego (which is not uncommon for most new 2LTs) and rub some NCOs and non-academy graduates the wrong way. My advice is do not be that guy or gal. An invitation to attend West Point should be treated as an honor and a privilege.

Reserve Officer Training Corps (ROTC)

ROTC provides college students with the ability to train to become Army officers. In ROTC, the curriculum includes elective leadership and military courses that help them become effective officers once they join the Army. The majority of newly commissioned 2LTs come from ROTC each year.

Requirements

To enroll in Army ROTC you must be:

- Accepted or enrolled in one of more than 700 participating colleges or universities
- A U.S. citizen
- Physically Fit and able to pass an Army Physical Fitness Test (APFT) on a "regular" basis
- Between the ages of 17 and 35

Advantages

The choice is outstanding because a wide selection of colleges offer ROTC. Almost all major colleges and most mid-to-major schools offer an ROTC program. You can sign a four-year contract (freshman to senior) or wait and sign a two-year contract (junior-senior). I recommend waiting until your sophomore or junior year to contract because it allows you time to get the "freshman follies" out of your system before you make a commitment to the Army.

Disadvantages

ROTC can pose very interesting social challenges on a college campus. As a cadet you represent the American soldier to the rest of the students on campus. You could become the target for anti-war rallies or other anti-military protests. Also, ROTC can be considered Army "light." Your instructors are professional and competent but the environment is nothing like what you would experience as an active duty officer. Advance camp places cadets in an Army field environment, but it only lasts a few weeks before you return to college for your senior year. If you sign a two-year contract, you will attend an additional six-week "basic" camp between your sophomore and junior years. This lack of experience in a regular Army environment can cause problems for some people after you are commissioned.

Officer Candidate School (OCS)

Officer Candidate School (OCS) is another way you can become an officer in the Army. After completing Basic Combat Training you participate in rigorous training for 12 weeks and then attend the Officer Basic Course (also known as Basic Officer Leaders Course II). The reserve component offers a 9-week fast track course and a traditional program offered over two 15-day annual training periods and 12 months of drill weekends.

Requirements

In order to attend Officer Candidate School you must be a U.S. citizen and a college graduate, at least 19 years old, and not have passed your 29th birthday at the time of selection. (Age waivers may be considered up to 41, 364 days upon commissioning.)

Advantages

Most OCS graduates have served time as enlisted soldiers. Depending on how far they rose in the enlisted ranks and how good of a Soldier they are, their credibility can be much higher than an Academy graduate or an ROTC graduate. However, no matter how good of an enlisted soldier they were, upon commissioning, they are just another "butter bar"—slang for a new 2LT wearing his gold rank insignia.

Disadvantages

Breaking the habits of a good NCO can be difficult. Staying in the "Officer Lane" is something a good number of former NCOs who earn a commission struggle with. There is also the potential physical problems of being older than most of your peers. Being in your late 20s is really not an issue, but 35-year-old lieutenants stand out. Most older NCOs can hang tough with their younger counterparts, but it takes them a little longer to recover. However, older officers often offer good leadership qualities like patience and the overall ability to deal with stress.

Direct Commission

Soldiers are eligible for direct-commissioning opportunities as medical professionals, lawyers, or chaplains. Direct commissioning is available in other job areas of the Army such as in the combat support and combat service support branches. Rank upon direct commission depends upon experience and skill level.

Requirements

- A degreed professional
- Within age requirements (varies by professional career field)
- A U.S. citizen
- Physically fit

Advantages

The service support branch is full of areas where a lot of commissioning training will be lost on a soldier who is going to be a lawyer or a medical doctor. Recruiting soldiers who already have the skills or who are capable of learning these valuable skills make the Army more self-sufficient and stronger. There are also many opportunities for Judge Advocate Generals (JAGs) and medical and chaplain personnel to earn lucrative bonuses because of the current needs of the Army.

Disadvantages

In some cases soldiers earn a direct commission in branches other than service support. All other commissioning sources are steeped in the 8 Troop Leading Procedures and OPORD creation, not to mention land navigation and infantry tactics. Without having this training, an officer will be behind the learning curve in combat. Combat is not the place for a leader to learn how to do his/her job.

OCS Courses

Federal OCS

Active Duty OCS is a 12-week course offered at Fort Benning, Georgia, in three distinct phases. Classes are offered year-round. The Program of Instruction (POI) is based on infantry company operations.

State OCS

Reserve Component OCS and National Guard is a 12- to 15-month (traditional) or 9-week (fast track) Leaders' Course of Instruction taught in a high-stress environment. This allows the cadre to develop and evaluate the performance of the candidates as it relates to their potential for commissioning as second lieutenants. The POI is based on infantry company operations.

Traditional: Phase I takes 16 days and is part of the candidates' annual training. After completion at a consolidated training site, candidates return to their home state to complete the 12-month Phase II at the state's Regional Training Institute (or RTI). Thereafter, candidates again use up their annual training for the 16-day consolidated Phase III. Once candidates successfully complete this final phase they are eligible for commissioning as a second lieutenant within their home state.

Fast Track: The fast track option is typically offered to candidates who are pushing the age limit or those who display the necessary tools and experience to become a second lieutenant in a shorter period of time. Fast track is offered at various RTIs throughout the National Guard. South Dakota, Alabama, and Pennsylvania are the only RTIs that currently offer fast track OCS. However, all states and territories can send candidates to these schools as long as the candidate's packets are prepared correctly.

During the fast track program, the three phases are broken down into a one-week reception, two-week Phase I, four-week Phase II, and a two-week Phase III. Upon completion, candidates are sent back to their home unit for commissioning.

Chapter 2

Requirements for Commissioning

"Be what you are. This is the first step toward becoming better than you are."

— Julius Hare

The standards required of an Officer Candidate are of the highest order. Your integrity of character must be an inspiration to others, and your conduct at all times must be above reproach. Personal appearance, military bearing, and military courtesy must be of the highest standard at all times.

Officer Candidates must meet the following standards necessary for graduation from OCS. These standards are also outlined in the Phase 1 Initial Counseling with an attached Student Evaluation Plan.

(1) ACADEMICS: Candidates cannot fail more than three written exams. A third written exam failure will result in academic probation. A fourth failure will result in a recommendation to the battalion commander for possible relief from the course. The candidate must be counseled on a DA 4856 [Department of the Army Counseling Form] of the consequences of the academic probation.

(2) LEADERSHIP: Serve in various command positions during all phases of training and achieve an overall satisfactory leadership rating.

(3) MORAL CHARACTER: Each Officer Candidate must have a high moral character, which is a necessity for a commissioned officer.

(4) MEDICAL: Each Officer Candidate must pass a physical examination as prescribed for appointment as an officer in AR 40-501. [Army Regulation that describes physical requirements.]

(5) PHYSICAL FITNESS: Each Officer Candidate must score a minimum of 60 points on each event of the Army Physical Fitness Test (APFT) with a minimum total score of 180 points. A large portion of the OCS environment is physical conditioning and requires stamina. Each Officer Candidate must participate in scheduled physical training. Candidates must complete all foot marches within recommended Army standards. During the Basic Phase, candidates will complete a 5-mile foot march. During the Intermediate Phase, candidates must complete a 7- and 10-mile foot march. Candidates who fail to meet the standard might be allowed one retest.

(6) WEIGHT STANDARDS: All Officer Candidates must meet the weight standards as published in AR 600-9, which can be found online.

(7) ATTENDANCE: Candidates who miss or cannot actively participate in 12 or more hours of scheduled training may be recommended for recycle, i.e., sent back to repeat the course.

Officer Candidates must meet all prerequisite requirements prior to enrollment in each phase of training as outlined in the current Course Management Plan and appropriate National Guard Bureau (NGB) or Army correspondence. Officer Candidates must also meet commissioning requirements, per AR 600-100 and appropriate

National Guard Bureau or Army correspondence. Officer Candidates not able to meet those standards must process a request for waiver. Waivers must be requested prior to enrollment in OCS. Officer Candidates will be counseled on both waiver approval or disapproval procedures for all waivers submitted by their unit or TAC chain of command.

Chapter 3

Packet Preparation

"When you pay for your experience, make sure you keep the receipt."

— Tyler Brinkman

Education Requirements

If you have a four-year degree you're eligible to apply to OCS. Until October 1, 2009, candidates could enter State OCS programs with only 60 credit hours and commission with 90 credits while Federal and Fast Track OCS allowed candidates to enter and commission with only 90 credits. With the current operational tempo, new Second Lieutenants would have 36 months (time before eligibility for Captain) to finish their bachelor's degree, Officer Basic Course, and in some cases a deployment to a forward area. A large number of officers would stall at the rank of First Lieutenant because of the lack of a bachelor's degree.

The new requirement of a four-year degree should allow newly commissioned lieutenants to focus on their officer basic course and unit operations to learn their position and simultaneously minimize the number of first lieutenants not suitable for promotion.

Commanders Letter of Recommendation (LOR)

All candidates need to have a letter of recommendation from an officer. It is always preferable to get a letter from an officer you have worked for and someone with the rank of captain or above. However, any officer from any branch of the service will suffice.

Most officers will gladly write a LOR for candidates if you show genuine promise. (See Appendix D for an example of a LOR.)

Security Clearance

In order to earn a commission as a second lieutenant, you must have the ability to earn a secret clearance. Depending on the branch of service you select, this requirement may be as high as top secret. You will fill out the electronic personnel security questionnaire (EPSQ) and submit it during phase zero of OCS. Typically, once the unit approves your request to attend OCS, the EPSQ packet should be started. In lieu of the EPSQ computer based program, you can get the process going by filling out a SF-86 by hand.

Below are some common reasons (but not all the reasons) why requests for security clearance can be denied:

- The applicant has been convicted in a U.S. court for a crime and a sentence of imprisonment for a term exceeding one year.
- The applicant is an unlawful user of, or is addicted to, a controlled substance (as defined in Section 102 of the Controlled Substances Act, 21 USC 802).
- The applicant is mentally incompetent, as determined by a mental health professional approved by the DoD.
- The applicant has been discharged or dismissed from the armed forces under dishonorable conditions.
- Bad credit history for a variety of reasons.

An interim secret clearance is awarded for most second lieutenants until the background check process is complete. However, an interim clearance can raise a red flag and hamper your promotion. It is best to address any blemish on your record as soon as possible.

Biography

An OCS biography is a record of your life up to the time you were accepted into the OCS program. Writing this is easier than it sounds. However, this is one of the most misunderstood part of the OCS packet. Candidates tend to make one of two mistakes:

> 1. Putting off the biography until the last minute, and then turning it in with errors, failing to communicate effectively to the reader (their TAC) why they want to be a commissioned officer.
>
> 2. They get too personal and write about things that raise red flags. Examples of things not to include in your biography include, but are not limited to: nicknames, fraternity or sorority stories, failures, important people you know, opinions about politics or current events, divorces, bankruptcies, arrests, your college GPA, or anything else that could offend someone or cause the spotlight to shine brightly on your name.

In short, keep it simple! Include your name, where you were born, some basic information about your family, your education and military experience (if any), and finally why you want to be an officer in the U.S. Army. Using this basic outline, most applicants have no problem filling at least one page, double-spaced with 12-point font.

One last thing: include a professional-looking picture for the biography. It is preferable to use the photo taken in Class A uniform, completely sterile with your OCS rank on it or in sterile Army Combat Uniforms (ACUs). DO NOT use a photo of you and your buddies from a night on the town for your biography photo. (Yes, some people do this. See mistake #2 above.) For more about writing your biography, see Appendix E.

Chapter 4

TAC Introduction

"Endure and persist. The pain will do you good."

— OVID

The Teach, Assess, Counsel method, or "TAC Attack"—the initial introduction to the TAC officers and TAC NCOs who will train you—is one of the most notorious and anticipated events in OCS. It begins with a motivational speech by a high-ranking officer, typically the regimental commander. At the end of the pep talk candidates are marched on to a parade field where their TACs await. In my case, a bagpipe version of Amazing Grace blared over the public address system. As soon as it concluded, the TAC Attack ensued.

Pieces of TA-50 (equipment soldiers wear) are slung everywhere, TACs yell out commands, and candidates are "smoked." TACs use this time to identify leaders and followers. Therefore, it benefits a candidate to step up and take charge. If you are tagged as a leader, TACs will order you to take charge of your element (platoon, squad, or team) and move it somewhere. The catch is that you will need to move your element in accordance with the field manual for Drill and Ceremony. Since few can move an element properly at this stage of the training—down you go and another will be selected to take your place. If no candidates are determined to be leadership material or volunteer to move an element, the TACs will gladly take charge of the element—and begin a smoke session from hell.

This will go on for one to two hours. Most of the non-hackers (less determined soldiers) quit within the first hour. Those who hang tough and survive the TAC attack are marched to their barracks and put through a full barracks inspection for contraband, read the integrity rules for OCS, and officially in-briefed and introduced to their platoon TACs. At this point candidate leadership is assigned and the rating period for the first leadership cycle begins.

Stressors

TACs are not allowed to curse or physically assault candidates, but yelling is completely authorized. The stress you will feel is natural and you should expect it. The TACs will deprive you of sleep, order you to do things within strict time constraints, and give you a task with little guidance on how to complete it. All this is designed to produce a high stress environment to get you used to operating under difficult conditions. It will train you to focus and operate under circumstances that approach the stress you might feel while in a combat zone. This is critical for training future officers. Anyone can make a decision under ideal conditions. During OCS you will be required to make decisions under extreme stress, which in turn trains future leaders to make competent decisions during less than ideal situations. Remember: everything is done for a reason during OCS. If you accept that premise, everything thrown at you will be easier to deal with.

Time Hacks

You will be given an order by the TACs to prepare for an inspection in one hour. In a perfect world, with a good chain of command, this task is completely achievable. At OCS, with perfect strangers from different backgrounds and aptitudes, this hour will fly by in what seems like just minutes. The goal of strict time hacks is to get the unit to work as a team to complete tasks in a timely manner.

TACs will never ask you to perform a task in an undetermined timeframe or an impossible timeframe. Successful completion of all tasks rest solely on candidate leadership and candidate followership.

Make a Decision

Always remember that during OCS, making a wrong decision is better than not making a decision at all. Aggressive mistakes are acceptable and trainable. Freezing up and neglecting or refusing to make any decision will get soldiers killed in combat and get leaders fired at OCS. Do not freeze up when a decision needs to be made. OCS is a controlled environment and is where mistakes need to be made. It's OK to make mistakes now and then so you learn from them. However, if you repeat the same mistake more than once, be prepared to hear about it from your TACs.

Dining Facility Procedures

Prior to each meal in the dining facility (DFAC) you will be expected to know what is on the menu, ground your equipment, perform the "exercise of the day," wash your hands, and ingest your nutritious meal as quickly as humanly possible. While the procedures differ slightly depending on where and when you attend OCS, the method behind the madness is all the same: attention to details. Typically, the DFAC procedure operates like this:

- The 1SG marches the company to the DFAC and turns the formation over to the CO.
- The CO asks the XO to "read the menu."
- The XO reads the menu. (Some OC Guides instruct candidates to echo "mmm" or "yum" as certain food items are read from the menu.)
- The CO asks for the candidate chaplain to bless the meal.

- The CO asks the Sr. TAC for the numbers. (The numbers are in reference to how many of the "exercises of the day" need to be performed by candidates prior to entering the DFAC.)
- The CO repeats the numbers to the company and gives the order of chow. Example: 1st PLT, 2nd PLT, 3rd PLT.
- The CO turns the company over to his/her platoon leaders then moves out, eating only after all his/her soldiers have eaten.

The procedures are simple. Executing the DFAC procedures takes about two minutes from beginning to end. However, if you cannot remember the procedures it can and will turn into a 25-minute smoke session. The TACs have a tight schedule and candidates have to eat, so the smoke session will end—but it can restart during any break in training. Learn the procedures before shipping to OCS. Each OCS location will post its Officer Candidate Guide on their web page. Get it and begin studying as soon as possible. You should also closely watch other candidates while you are not acting in a leadership role. Learn from their mistakes so you do not repeat them.

Smoke Sessions

The origin of the term "smoke session" is the act of pushing your body so hard physically that the heat coming off your body (sweat) steams in colder weather and looks like smoke. If you attend boot camp and the weather drops below 55 degrees while you or someone else is getting "smoked" by your drill sergeant, you will see it firsthand.

TAC's will "bring smoke" on candidates initially during the TAC Attack and then after when mental or physical mistakes are made. Don't worry—they don't last indefinitely and to date, no candidates have ever died during a smoke session. The smoke sessions are used to motivate you. If you or another candidate repeat mistakes or are not learning from prior mistakes (to the satisfaction of a TAC), it must be a motivation issue because the training is comprehensive. Getting smoked will motivate you. In most cases you will be tired much of the time and often feel lethargic due to the rigorous schedule and lack of sleep. A smoke session gets the blood flowing and will put a little pep in your step. It is strong motivation to learn from your mistakes so that you become a better officer. The threat of smoke sessions adds stress to your environment, which in turn improves the overall OCS training climate.

Chapter 5

Course Work

"Military history is the most effective way of training during peacetime."

— Von Moltke

Regardless of where you attend OSC, the materials you will cover from the beginning of your training until the end will be the same (although the order of coverage might change). The Course Management Program (CMP) and Program of Instruction (POI) were created by Fort Benning OCS. Each Regional Training Institute (RTI) is reviewed every two years to ensure it is training officer candidates according to the standards set forth by Fort Benning OCS. This helps ensure that commissioning second lieutenants from every state and territory are held to the same rigorous standards regardless of where they received their instruction.

The following list represents the most current required knowledge and training topics covered in OCS (organized by phase).

Required Knowledge

There are four required knowledge items. If you study these in advance, along with the eight troop leading procedures (TLPs) and the five-paragraph Operational Order (OPORD) format, the odds are you will not be the candidate doing extra exercise before meals. Memorize them now! Learn how they apply as you move along in training so you are comfortable with them, and will know in advance when to expect them.

Chain of Command

Commander in Chief
Secretary of Defense
Secretary of the Army
Chairman, Joint Chiefs of Staff
Army Chief of Staff
TRADOC Commander
Commandant
USAIS Assistant Commandant or NGB Chief of Staff
USAIS Commander / State Adjutant General
Brigade Commander
Regimental Commander
Battalion Commander
(OCS) Company Commander
Senior Training Officer
Platoon Training Officer

General Orders

1. I will guard everything within the limits of my post and quit my post only when properly relieved.

2. I will obey my special orders and perform all my duties in a military manner.

3. I will report violations of my special orders, emergencies, and anything not covered in my instructions to the Commander of the Relief.

Soldiers' Creed

I am an American Soldier.
I am a Warrior and a member of a team.
I serve the people of the United States and live the Army Values.
I will always place the mission first.
I will never accept defeat.
I will never quit. I will never leave a fallen comrade.
I am disciplined, physically and mentally tough, trained and proficient in my warrior tasks and drills.
I always maintain my arms, my equipment and myself.
I am an expert and I am a professional.
I stand ready to deploy, engage, and destroy the enemies of the United States of America in close combat.
I am a guardian of freedom and the American way of life.
I am an American Soldier.

OCS Honor Code

An Officer Candidate will not lie, cheat, steal, or tolerate those who do.

Phase Zero / Pre-OCS Training

- Map Reading
- Land Navigation
- Drill and Ceremony
- Troop Leading Procedures

Key components to land navigation are listed below:

1. Back Azimuth
   A. Greater than 180 degrees subtract 180
   B. Less than 180 degrees add 180

2. G-M Angle Conversion

A. Westerly G-M Angle
(1) Grid to Magnetic: Add G-M Angle
(2) Magnetic to Grid: Subtract G-M Angle

B. Easterly G-M Angle
(1) Grid to Magnetic: Subtract G-M Angle
(2) Magnetic to Grid: Add G-M Angle

3. INTERSECTION: To Locate an Unknown Point

A. Orient Map Using Compass
B. Locate and Mark Your Position on the Map
C. Determine Magnetic Azimuth From Your Position to Unknown Point Using Compass
D. Convert the Magnetic Azimuth to a Grid Azimuth
E. Plot the Grid Azimuth From Your Position in the Direction of the Unknown Point
F. Move to a Second Known Position and Repeat Steps c, d, e.
G. The Unknown Point is Where the Lines Intersect on the Map

4. RESECTION: To Locate Your Own Position

A. Orient Map Using Compass
B. Locate Two Known Points on the Ground and Mark Them on Your Map
C. Measure the Magnetic Azimuth to one of the Known Locations
D. Convert the Magnetic Azimuth to a Grid Azimuth
E. Convert the Grid Azimuth to a Back Azimuth
F. Use a Protractor to Plot the Azimuth and Draw a Line From the Known Point to Your Location
G. Repeat Steps c, d, e, f For the Second Known Point
H. Your Location is Where the Lines Cross

Basic or Phase I Training

(This can vary depending of whether it is State vs. Federal)

Staff Activities
Troop Leading Procedures
Oral Operations Orders
Customs of the Service
Leadership Doctrine
Train an Individual Task
Risk Assessments
Train a Team
Train a Squad
Team Development
Implement PT Program
Duties and Responsibilities
Map Reading
Land Navigation (Intermediate Federal)

Intermediate or Phase II

Principles of War
Intro to Combat Operations
Defensive Tactics
Army Organization
Branch Information
Tactical Radio
Tactical Phone
Intro to Fire Support
Call/Adjust Fire
Preventative Medicine
Supply Activities
Admin/Personnel Actions
Report Casualties
Physical Security
Military Justice

Small Unit Combat Operations
Conduct PMCS
Financial Readiness
Leadership Doctrine
Leadership Ethics
Ethical Decision Making
Communicate Effectively
Counsel a Subordinate
EO/Sexual Harrassment
Code of Conduct
Operational Security
Protect Classified Information
Integrate Threat Capabilities
Physical Security
Process Captives
Implement PT Program
Conduct Drill and Ceremony
Suicide Prevention
Host Nations
Integrate Military History
Write in the Army Style
Military Briefings

Senior or Phase III

Leadership Reaction Course
Tactical Leadership Course
Training Without Troops (TEWT)
Field Leadership Exercise

Federal OCS: Phase I typically is reception week for Fort Benning candidates. Packets are finalized and an APFT is administered. Familiarization with the OCS Guide is crucial during this time.

State OCS: This phase is 3-6 months of drill weekends and consists of instruction in basic soldier skills, drill and ceremony, physical training, and administrative preparation. The goal is to prepare prospective candidates to succeed in OCS.

Overall Suggested Training:

Map Reading: This is a refresher for most candidates. If you have not read a map in a while, get with a good soldier who can give you some refresher training.

Drill and Ceremony: Marching soldiers to and from training events will happen daily. A good cadence caller will motivate all candidates. The opposite is also true.

Physical Training: Get into Army shape. (See Appendix F.)

OC Guide: Each OCS training regiment has its own guide. Get your hands on it and begin learning the rules.

Introduction to OCS Environment: Hopefully your pre-OCS instructor is a qualified TAC. Prior to departing for Phase I, a short "TAC introduction" should be performed to get you acclimated to what is in store.

Injury Prevention: Getting in Army shape will help. If you are older than 35, your body will take a little more repetition to help reduce the likelihood of injury. Put in the extra work! Getting recycled from OCS due to injury is not likely, but it does happen. Do what you can now so it is less likely to happen to you.

Phases & Gates

OCS is broken down into distinct phases. While Federal OCS does not identify phases, there are specific gates in the schedule that allow injured candidates to recycle back to the gate or phase instead of starting over. Each "phase" has different learning objectives, goals, and priorities. Each phase of OCS varies slightly depending upon where you attend OCS. A description of each phase is listed below.

Pre-Week 1

Reserve Component: This is very similar to reception for boot camp. Small items missing from packets can be finalized and a "last chance" APFT can be given. However, if you arrive at Ft. Benning without a complete packet, your chain of command has failed you; be prepared to suffer for it!

State: If drilling with state RTI, Week 1 should be very similar to Phase I. The intent is simple: inflict stress upon you to get you acclimated to Phase I, Day One. Packets should also be reviewed one last time and any "last chance" APFT should be assigned.

Phase I

Federal: The Basic Phase begins with individual skills training. You will be shown the OCS standards by the cadre and expected to meet them. As you progress through the course, you will be given increased responsibility and work to integrate individual skills into collective tasks and missions.

State: Consists of one 16-day annual training period. Training focuses on the individual, squad, and platoon levels. Candidates receive military subject, land navigation, and leadership training under high stress conditions. During Phase I you will maintain a climate of strict discipline as the cadre shows you OCS standards and then expects you to meet these standards. You and your fellow candidates will train under extremely demanding mental and physical conditions.

Phase II

Federal: Intermediate phase is classroom heavy and consists of many written exams, including a major gate: Land Navigation. The Land Navigation bank of exams consist of a written exam with a day and night Land Navigation course. Failure on either one can result in you being recycled or dismissed from the course. Phase I represents the "starting" phase of team-building. Phase II is the "norming" phase where teams are built, SOPs are created, and a predictable operating tempo is achieved.

State: In the traditional program, Phase II occurs during IDT weekends between the first and second annual training periods. In the Accelerated Program, Phase II is a four-week ADT period.

Phase II is characterized by increased TAC officer teaching and a slight reduction in stress producing situations. Training focuses on the individual, squad, and platoon levels. During this phase you will continue to perfect the skills learned in the basic phase and strive for tactical and small unit leadership skills and confidence. You will assume additional responsibilities designed to refine your leadership skills through additional challenges of maintaining a completely functional student chain of command. Academically speaking, you will be taught and tested in subjects including Tactics, Operations, Military Intelligence, Military Justice, Field Artillery, and more.

IDT (drill) status with your home state's training regiment.

Phase III or Senior Phase

Federal: This phase includes advanced leadership studies and scenarios with an emphasis on officership and self-development. You will participate in senior leadership seminars and social events during this phase. The senior phase is your final opportunity to refine your officer skills to prepare you for the officer environment.

State: Consists of one 16-day annual training period. Training occurs at individual, squad, and platoon level with the focus on tactical operations and field leadership. The TAC officer role is that of a teacher, mentor, and role model. This phase is the final refining of the candidate done by the cadre to ultimately prepare the candidate for the officer environment.

Staff Ride

"Staff rides represent a unique and persuasive method of conveying the lesson of the past to the present-day Army leadership for current application. Properly conducted, these exercises bring to life, on the very terrain where historic encounters took place, examples, applicable today as in the past, of leadership tactics and strategy, communications, use of terrain, and, above all, the psychology of men in battle. This historical study, particularly with personal reconnaissance, offers valuable opportunities to develop professional leader ship and the capacity for effective use of combined arms on the air-land battlefield."

— William Glenn Robertson, Director, U.S. Army's Combat Studies Institute, U.S. Army Combined Arms Center, Fort Leavenworth, Kansas

Staff rides are common for Officer Candidate School, but are not a requirement of the CMP. I have had the opportunity to take part in four staff rides, one as an Officer Candidate, one as a Lieutenant, and two as a TAC. Each one was well worth the time and effort and I learned many interesting things during each trip. It may seem unrealistic, but many of the tactics, techniques, and procedures (TTPs) used by the Civil War-era army are still in use today. Walking battlefields provided a greater understanding of what the leadership of that day was up against and the considerations leaders needed to make to be successful. You cannot get this realism from a book or a movie.

In my opinion, the Staff Ride should become part of the CMP for all military training from the rank of E-5 Sergeant through the Command and General Staff College (CGSC). The information derived from past military operations is invaluable. Regardless of where you are in your officer career, accept any opportunity you have to participate in a staff ride. You never know when what you learn during the staff ride will come in handy for you and the soldiers under your command.

Chapter 6

Physical Training

"If we exercise now, how much stronger we will be when the test comes!"

—William James

You Are in Charge

TAC Officers and NCOs do not lead Physical Training (PT) like during basic training and in normal line units. At OCS, the candidates are in charge of PT from beginning to end. This means creating a PT plan to include risk assessments, warm-up, stretching, main event, and cool down. Don't get too ambitions with the plan because if you go over the allotted time the rest of your day will get behind. Always keep in mind that each day is very strictly scheduled.

A challenging and well organized PT session shows good leadership and organization skills. (Keep in mind that the opposite also applies.) Below are some examples of simple yet challenging PT sessions:

- A 25-minute run split up by ability groups.
- PT consisting of 8 to 12 total body exercises station set on a two-minute rotation.
- Grass drills (3- to 5-second rushes, low crawl, and high crawl).
- Competition between squads or platoon, if allowed.

Below is an example of a PT schedule I used while a platoon leader. It is a five-day weekly PT schedule. You may not have time to put together something on a computer, but simply printing off a calendar and plugging in exercises will make life easier on you and your classmates.

	January 3, 2005	**January 4, 2005**	**January 5, 2005**	**January 6, 2005**	**January 7, 2005**
WEEK ONE	A: Ability Group Run	A: Pushups / Sit-ups Pyramid	A: TBD	A: Partner-Resisted Exercises	A: Ability Group Run
	D: 3 MIL	D: 1 Hr	D: 1 Hr	D: 1 Hr	D: 3 MIL
	L: PRT 108	L: Davidson	L: PRT 108	L: Davidson	L: PRT 108
	I: LOW-MED	I: Med-High	I: High	I: High	I: Med-High
	January 10, 2005	**January 11, 2005**	**January 12, 2005**	**January 13, 2005**	**January 14, 2005**
WEEK TWO	A: Ability Group Run	A: Circuit Training P/U, S/U Improvement	A: TBD	A: Guerilla / Grass Drills	A: Ability Group Run
	D: 3.5 Mil	D: 1 Hr	D: 1 Hr	D: 1 Hr	D: 3.5 MIL
	L: PRT 108	L: Davidson	L: PRT 108	L: PRT 108	L: PRT 108
	I: LOW-MED	I: High	I: High	I: Med-High	I: Med-High

	January 17, 2005	January 18, 2005	January 19, 2005	January 20, 2005	January 21, 2005
WEEK THREE	No PT	No PT	No PT	A:Pushups / Sit-ups Pyramid / Short Run	A: Ability Group Run
	Weapons Range	Weapons Range	Weapons Range	D: 1 Hr	D: 4 MIL
				L: Davidson	L: PRT 108
				I: Med-High	I: Med-High
	January 24, 2005	**January 25, 2005**	**January 26, 2005**	**January 27, 2005**	**January 28, 2005**
WEEK FOUR	A:Class Run	A:Pushups / Sit-ups Pyramid/ Sprints	A: Ability Group Run	A: Circuit Training Cardio. Endurance	A: Ability Group Run
	D: 4.5 MIL	D: 1 Hr	D: 1 Hr	D: 1 Hr	D: 5 MIL
	L: PRT 108	L: Davidson	L: PRT 108	L: Davidson	L: PRT 108
	I: LOW-MED	I: Med-High	I: High	I: High	I: High
	January 31, 2005	**February 1, 2005**	**February 2, 2005**	**February 3, 2005**	**February 4, 2005**
WEEK FIVE	A: Class Run	A: Circuit Training Strength Development	A: Ability Group	Stretching	No PT
	D: 5 MIL	D: 1 Hr	D: 3 Mil	Height / Weight	Mid Course
	L: PRT 108	L: Davidson	L: PRT 108		APFT
	I: LOW-MED	I: Med-High	I: Low		

Foot Marches

In order to graduate OCS, you will need to complete a five-, seven-, and ten-mile foot march while carrying at least a 35-pound rucksack. Candidate leadership will create a plan. An operations order (OPORD) may or may not be required depending on the school, but be prepared to create one. This plan should include:

- Risk assessment.
- Strip map with start and finish points, rest points, water points, location of medical aid.
- Marching order of company.
- Complete packing list.

Example Foot March Operations Order (OPORD)

Below is an Operations Order (OPORD) created by one of my candidates in 2009 for the 10-mile foot march. State traditional OCS use three-day weekend drills over a 12-14 month period to meet the Phase II POI established by Fort Benning. The format is sound, but keep in mind that some of the information contained within this OPORD is relevant only to this particular mission.

OCS Class 52 1BN (GS) 205 REG
Redmond Training Site, WA
121700JUN09 – 141700JUN09

Operations Order: 10-08 (OCS)

Time Zone: Pacific Standard

Task Organization: 1st Platoon, B/Co., is organized as a rifle platoon with two squads, each containing two fire teams.

1. Situation

a) Enemy Forces

1) Terrain: The training area contains classroom buildings and gradually sloping lawns bordered by woodlands and residential areas. It contains improved roads. Movement to and from the classroom, Dining Facility and Physical Fitness Training area should be unaffected by the terrain.

2) Foot March: The foot march will be a length of 10 miles and limited to 3.5 hours to complete. It will be conducted on the Sammamish River Trail, a route that is paved and should allow unobstructed movement.

3) Weather: The weather in Washington at this time of year is mild, but it is best to be prepared for rain so Officer Candidates will need to make sure that they have complete wet weather gear.

4) Time: Time will be a great factor and consideration in the success of the mission; both exams and foot march are timed events. All officer candidates are urged to move and train with a sense of urgency in order to meet timelines and complete all events successfully.

5) Civil Considerations: We will be training in close proximity with civilian residents, so quiet hours will be observed between 2200 hour and 0800 hours.

b) Friendly Forces

1)1st BN (GS) 205th Regiment (Leadership) Staff

a) To assist in mentorship and teaching of all Officer Candidates through instruction, example and physical exercises. Provide a training environment to develop leadership qualities and skills.

2) 1st Platoon

a) To continue through Phase II of the OCS program and develop the leadership qualities needed as a Second Lieutenant. OCS Class 52 will conduct tactical classroom and field training at or near the Redmond Training Site, WA NLT 121700JUN09.

c) Attachments and Detachments.
None
d) Assumptions
None

2. Mission

1st Platoon will conduct classroom and tactical field training at the Redmond Training Site, WA NLT 121700JUN09 IOT develop tactically sound leaders for the Washington Army National Guard.

3. Execution

Ensure 100% of candidates receive GOs on the 10-Mile Foot March, Army Physical Fitness Test and Military Intelligence Exam, and the platoon executes the training schedule effectively within the given timeline.

a) Concept of Operations
The mission will be conducted during the MUTA 5 drill weekend in accordance with the training schedule (Annex A).
1) Maneuver.
None
2) Fires.
None
3) Recon.
None
4) Intel.
None
5) Engineer
None
6) Air Defense
None
7) Information Ops.
None
b) Task to Maneuver Units

1) PSG, OC Ding

a) Task: Create 35-pound packing list for Ruck March (this should be done by the time the OPORD is posted for the platoon to view.)

b) Purpose: To ensure that Class 52 has a uniform standard for items being carried in rucksack.

2) SQD LDRs

a) Task: Report accountability status NLT 112200MAY09.

b) Purpose: To ensure that OCS Class 52 has proper accountability for drill weekend and to address any issues.

a) Task: Monitor and report out on squad member's progress with reading, book report assignment, and study for exam.

b) Purpose: To ensure that squad members are actively reading their copy of "On Combat" and receive all GO's on APFT, Foot March and Military Intilegence exam.

a) Task: Conduct pre-combat checks and pre-combat inspections on squad members.

b) Purpose: To ensure that all squad members meet the PSG guidance for packing list.

c) Coordinating Instructions

1) General Timeline

12 JUN 09 Conduct Training

13 JUN 09 Conduct Training

14 JUN 09 Conduct Training

2) Specific Timeline

12 JUN 09 (See Annex A. Training Schedule)

13 JUN 09 (See Annex A. Training Schedule)

14 JUN 09 (See Annex A. Training Schedule)

3) Commander's Critical Information. Examination NO GO's will require scheduling retesting, the weather could be a factor in causing heat or cold injuries, good time management is of utmost importance for training 12 JUN 09. Medical emergencies

4) Risk Reduction Control Measures. See daily risk assessments (Annex B)

5) Rules of Engagement

None

6) Environmental Considerations

(See Para. 1a)
7) MOPP level
Zero
8) Additional Instructions
None

4. Service and Support

a) Uniform: Identification Card
Identification Tags
ACU
Map Case
LBV
Kevlar
b) Health Service
1) CLS or medically trained soldier determines if injuries are life threatening.
2) Evacuation consists of two categories:
a) Life-threatening Plan
CLS or medically trained soldier determines if injuries are life-threatening.
b) If injuries are life-threatening, call 911.
3) Non Life-threatening Plan
a) CLS or medically trained soldier determines if injuries are life-threatening
b) If non-life threatening, evaluate transportation decision.
c) Meals: A-A-A

5. Command and Signal

a) Command
1) Officer Candidate Chain of Command
a) PL – OC Snuffy
b) PSG – OC Jones
c) 1SL – OC Park
d) 2SL – OC Smith
b) Signal

1) Phone and Email Communication
   a) PL, call sign "Wildcat 1-6" – OC Snuffy
   b) PSG, call sign "Wildcat 1-7" – OC Jones
   c) 1SL, call sign "Wildcat 1-1" – OC Park
   d) 2SL, call sign "Wildcat 1-2" – OC Smith

OFFICIAL:

SNUFFY, CANDIDATE
OC, Class 52
Platoon Leader

ANNEXES

A) Road March Strip Map
B) Directions to Road March Start Point

DISTRIBUTION

Senior TAC Officer
Class 52

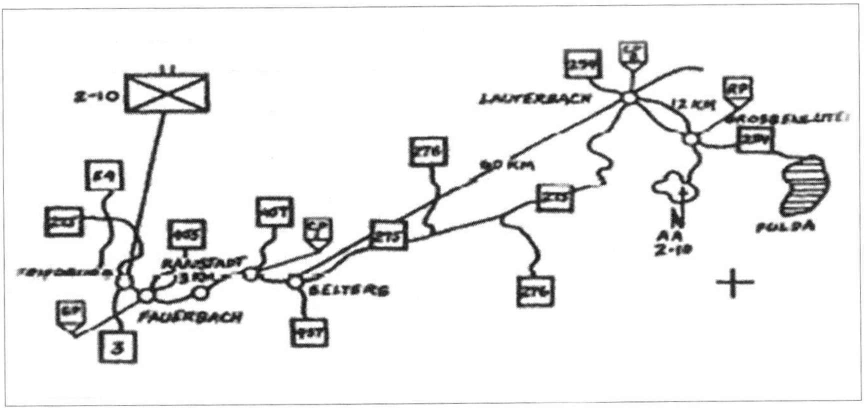

Example Strip Map

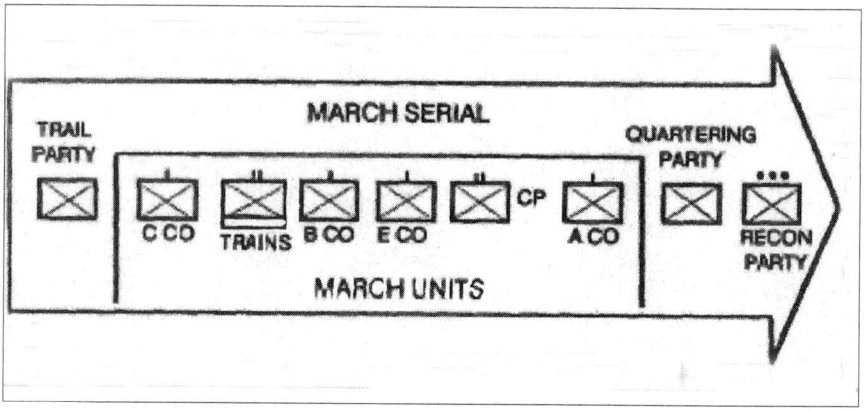

Example Marching Order

Physical Preparation for Foot March

Conditioning your feet, legs, and back is necessary to complete a foot march without having problems like blisters and cramps. Begin this conditioning by breaking in two good pairs of boots. Two pairs need to be broken in because you will use both during the 7- and 10-mile foot march. Purchasing a new expensive pair of boots is an option, but not necessary. A good pair of issue boots works fine if they are broken in properly. The simplest way to break in new boots is by wearing them.

One technique I have had success with while preparing for foot marches is doing a slow jog in boots and perform all practice foot marches in PT shoes. This way, you condition the foot to the boot without damaging your knees or back, and you will condition your legs and back with little undue stress to your feet.

Keep in mind that this is just one technique and not a hard and fast rule.

Below are recommendations from FM 21-18:

"Foot hygiene and sanitation are extremely important because your feet are enclosed in heavy rigid footwear during most working hours and are constantly in action. Foot care involves good hygiene measures such as frequent bathing, the use of foot powder, wearing properly fitted footwear to allow for ventilation, and correctly trimming your toenails.

Foot Hygiene

Do NOT overlook even the most minor of foot ailments. Always take good care of your feet. Many major conditions requiring hospitalization and disability come about because of neglect or mistreating your feet. Ignoring minor conditions will guarantee they become major problems.

Conditioning

Conditioning is accomplished by progressively increasing the distance you march each day. Marching is a good way to strengthen the feet and legs. Running alone will not suffice. The arch, ankle, and calf can be conditioned by performing simple exercises. For example, rising high on the toes or placing your feet on towels and using your toes to roll the towel back under the arch will condition your calf and feet muscles.

Preventative Measures

Certain preventive measures can be implemented to avoid painful foot problems.

Before marches: Trim your toenails at least every two or three weeks, depending upon your individual needs. Cut toenails short, square, and straight across. Keep your feet clean and dry and use foot powder. Wear clean, dry, good-fitting socks that have not been mended (and socks that are preferably cushion-soled) with seams and knots outside will keep your feet comfortable.

A nylon or polypropylene sock liner can reduce friction and add protection. Always carry an extra pair of socks, and carefully fit new boots with your socks. When you are getting used to a new pair of boots, alternate them with another pair and tape known hot spots on your feet before wearing them.

During halts: Lie down with your feet elevated every time there is a halt. If time permits, remove your boots and massage your feet, apply foot powder, change your socks, and medicate any blisters. This is very important if you have the time to do this.

Cover any open blisters, cuts, or abrasions with absorbent adhesive bandages. You can get some relief from swelling feet by slightly loosening your bootlaces where they cross the arch of your foot.

After marches: Repeat the care procedures for your feet, wash and dry your socks, and dry out your boots. Medicate blisters, abrasions, corns, and calluses. Inspect painful feet for sprains and improper fitting of socks and boots. Prolonged marching can make your feet red, swollen, and tender along the sides, and these areas can become blisters. Aerate your feet, elevate them, rest them, and try to get wider footwear if possible.

Keeping your feet clean will prevent major problems later. For example, small amounts of dirt can form blisters by rubbing against your skin, and perspiration can cause infection. If possible, wash your feet each day. When you are in the field, use cool water to reduce heat, irritation, and some swelling. Make sure your feet are dry before putting your socks and boots back on."

These recommendations are very important, but there is a catch: you will not have much time for them at Federal or State OCS. Do whatever you can, when you can. If you develop problems, medics will always be available to check your feet after marches.

Chapter 7

Rating Scheme

"Never discourage anyone who continually makes progress, no matter how slow."

— Plato

OCS Candidates are evaluated in all company leadership positions. (Chapter 16 has more detail about the specific roles of each rate leadership position). The positions are as follows:

Company Level

- Company Commander (CO)
- Executive Officer (XO)
- First Sergeant (1SG)

Platoon Level

- Platoon Leader (PL)
- Platoon Sergeant (PSG)
- Three to four Squad Leaders (SL's)
- Six to eight Team Leaders (TL's)

Rating periods typically last 24 to 48 hours or an entire weekend during State OCS. You will be given a proper in-brief that focuses on the position you will hold and the critical events and expectations during your rated period. If you fail to earn a satisfactory rating during your time in leadership, you will be given another chance. If you regress or fail to improve during your next rated period, TAC staff can begin the process necessary to remove or recycle you from / through the OCS program.

Leadership in Brief (Blue Card): The position summary will be covered followed by critical events and expectations for your time in leadership. This shows you exactly what you will be rated on by your TAC. During the in-brief is when the TAC is usually open to questions. Make the most of it! Remember to wait until the end of the in-brief before you ask any questions.

LEADERSHIP EVALUATION IN-BRIEF					
PART I - ADMINISTRATIVE DATA					
CANDIDATE NAME (Last, First, MI)	LAST 4	CO/PLT/SQD	PHASE	DATE	POSITION
RATER'S NAME / RANK / POS		FROM: DAY / MONTH / YEAR		TO: DAY / MONTH / YEAR	
PART II - EXPLANATION OF RATING SYSTEM					
SCALE OVERALL NET ASSESSMENT (Circle one) E (Excellent) S (Satisfactory) N (Not Satisfactory)					
PART III – DUTY DESCRIPTION					
PART IV - CRITICAL EVENTS / EXPECTATIONS					

(FRONT)

LEADERSHIP EVALUATION IN BRIEF	
PART V - SUMMARY Date and Summary of Counseling: Candidate's Comments on Expectations:	
Rater's Signature and Date:	Candidate's Signature and Date:

Spot Reports (Green Card): The Spot Reports are filled out by both the TAC and in some cases the candidate (you). The TAC uses the Spot Report (Green Card) to document your performance while in leadership. The Green Card is used to document performance during execution of critical events and expectations. In some cases, when you have done something outstanding or incorrectly, the TAC will order you to fill out a negative or positive spot report and deliver it back to the TAC within a specified period of time. The Green Card will help build the Leadership Evaluation Report for your rated period. A spot report will be filled out when you are in a leadership position and at times when you are not in a leadership position.

LEADERSHIP OBSERVATION REPORT Roster #

1. NAME (LAST, FIRST MI)	2. RANK	3. POSITION	4. PHASE	5. DATE

6. UNIT____ COMPANY _____PLT_____SQD NATURE OF REPORT:

7. LAST FOUR: LEADERSHIP/SPOT NEGATIVE/SPOT POSITIVE

ARMY VALUES / CORE LEADER COMPETENCIES / ATTRIBUTES

ARMY VALUES

Loyalty Duty Respect Selfless-Service Honor Integrity Personal Courage

CORE LEADER COMPETENCIES			ATTRIBUTES		
Leads Leads others Extends influence beyond the Chain of Command Leads by Example Communicates	Develops Creates a positive environment Prepares self Develops others	Achieves Gets Results	Leader of Character Army Values Empathy Warrior Ethos	Leader with Presence Military Bearing Physically Fit Composed, confident Resilient	Leader with Intellectual Capacity Mental agility Sound Judgment Innovation Interpersonal tact Domain knowledge

OBSERVATIONS AND REMARKS (TIME/EVENT/RESULTS)

ARNGOCS Form 3

OBSERVATION AND REMARKS (TIME/EVENT/RESULTS) CONT.

CORRECTIVE TRAINING/ COURSE OF ACTION TO BE TAKEN

CADRE SIGNATURE	DATE	CANDIDATE SIGNATURE	DATE

Self Evaluation (Yellow Card): You need to keep a log of what things you execute well, and what you do poorly. The Yellow Card provides the canvas for you to do just that. Everything is documented in the Time-Event-Result (TER) format. Some RTIs use STAR, TAR, TAR (Situation, Task, Activity, Result–Task, Activity, Result x 2).

CANDIDATE SELF-ASSESSMENT REPORT

CANDIDATE	CO / PLT	DUTY POSITION	DURATION	DATE
Birchfield, William J	A 2nd	PLT Leader	Feb IDT	02FEB06

SUMMARY OF PERFORMANCE (Give the Time, the Event, and the Result)

Time: 1105

Event: Formation to move to chow. I turned the platoon over to the platoon sergeant.

Result: The platoon sergeant took charge and took the platoon to chow.

Time: 1120

Event: Formation outside of dining facility. I was not in the proper position. CPT Ray asked me if I was 6 steps in front of the platoon.

Result: I corrected my position in the formation.

REFERENCE OC GUIDE

Field Leadership Evaluation Report (FLER Card): This rating document is used during squad and platoon training lanes. This card holds your commission in the balance. Anything less than an “S” on this card translates, at a minimum, to retraining or at worse, to recycling. (See next page for example.)

FIELD LEADERSHIP PERFORMANCE EVALUATION REPORT

CANDIDATE NAME (LAST, FIRST, MI)	LAST 4	CO/PLT/SQD	PHASE	DATE	POSITION

	E-S-N	TROOP LEADING PROCEDURES
RECEIVE THE MISSION		COMMENTS:
ISSUE WARNINGDER		COMMENTS:
MAKE A TENTATIVE PLAN		COMMENTS:
START NECESS. MVMNT		COMMENTS:
RECONNAISSANCE		COMMENTS:
COMPLETE PLAN		COMMENTS:
ISSUE OPORD		COMMENTS:
SUPERVISE / REFINE		COMMENTS:

E – EXCELLENT Exceeds requirements | S – SATISFACTORY Meets requirements | NI – NEEDS IMPROVEMENT Fails to meet requirements

OBSERVATIONS AND REMARKS

SUSTAIN

IMPROVE

SUMMARY

LEADERSHIP PERFORMANCE RATING

HIGH DEGREE ← E S N → LOW DEGREE

RATER NAME (LAST, FIRST MI), RANK	RATER SIGNATURE	DATE
CANDIDATE NAME (LAST, FIRST MI)	CANDIDATE SIGNATURE	DATE

Leadership Evaluation Reports (LERs): The LER looks very similar to an Officer Evaluation Report (OER). It uses the FM 6-22 Army Leadership manual as the main reference. The seven-page document allows the TAC to reflect on your core competencies and attributes during your time in a leadership position. On the last page is an overall evaluation (E-S-N) and summary with an optional plan for improvement and follow-up. You will find a seven-page example reproduced in Appendix C.

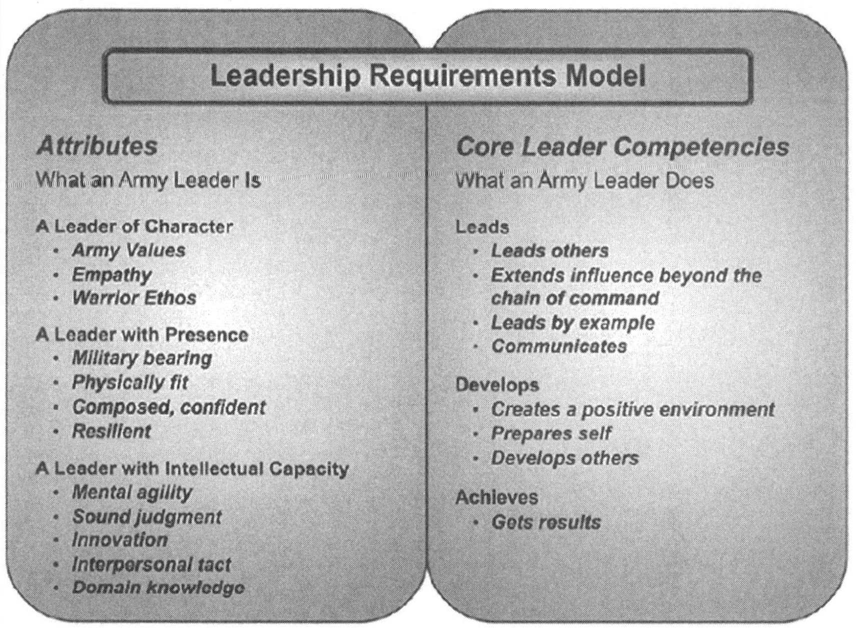

Leadership Requirements Model
Attributes
What an Army Leader Is
A Leader of Character
Army Values
Empathy
Warrior Ethos
A Leader with Presence
Military bearing
Physically fit
Composed, confident
Resilient
A Leader with Intellectual Capacity
Mental agility
Sound judgment
Innovation
Interpersonal tact
Domain knowledge
Core Leader Competencies
What an Army Leader Does
Leads
Leads others
Extends influence beyond the chain of command
Leads by example
Communicates
Develops
Creates a positive environment
Prepares self
Develops others
Achieves
Gets results

Core Leader Competencies

LEADS OTHERS Leaders motivate, inspire, and influence others to take initiative, work toward a common purpose, accomplish critical tasks, and achieve organizational objectives. Influence is focused on compelling others to go beyond their individual interest and to work for the common good.	
Establish and impart clear intent and purpose	Determines goals of objective. Determines the course of action (COA) necessary to reach objectives and fulfill mission requirements. Restates the higher headquarters mission in terms appropriate to the organization. Communicates instructions, orders, and directives to subordinates. Ensures subordinates understand and accept directions. Empowers and delegates authority to subordinates. Focuses the most important aspects of the situation.
Uses appropriate influence techniques to energize others	Uses techniques ranging from compliance to commitment (pressure, legitimate request, exchange, personal appeals, collaboration, rational persuasion, apprising, inspiration, participation, and relationship building).

Conveys the significance of the work	Inspires, encourages, and guides others toward mission accomplishment. When appropriate, explains how tasks support the mission and how missions support organizational objectives. Emphasizes the importance of organizational goals.
Maintains and enforces high professional standards	Reinforces the importance and role of standards. Performs individual and collective tasks to standard. Recognizes and takes responsibility for poor performance and addresses it appropriately.
Balances requirements of mission with welfare of followers	Assesses and routinely monitors the impact of mission fulfillment on mental, physical, and emotional attributes of subordinates. Monitors moral, physical condition, and safety of subordinates. Provides appropriate relief when conditions jeopardize success of the mission or present overwhelming risk to personnel.
Creates and promulgates vision of the future	Interprets data about the future environment, tasks, and missions. Forecast probable situations and outcomes and formulates strategies to prepare for them. Communicates to others the need for a greater understanding of the future environment, challenges, and objectives.

EXTENDS INFLUENCE	
Leaders need to influence beyond their direct lines of authority and beyond chains of command. This influence may extend to joint, interagency, intergovernmental, multinational, and other groups. In these situations, leaders use indirect means of influence: diplomacy, negotiation, mediation, arbitration, partnering, conflict resolution, consensus building, and coordination.	
Understands sphere of influence, means of influence, and limits of influence	Assesses situation, mission, and assignments to determine the parties involved in decision making, decision support, and possible interference or resistance.
Build trust	Is firm, fair, and respectful to gain trust. Identifies areas of commonality. Engages other members in activities and objectives. Follows through on actions related to expectations of others. Keeps people informed of actions and results.
Negotiates for understanding, builds consensus, and resolves conflict	Leverages trust to establish agreements and courses of action. Clarifies the situation. Identifies individual's and groups' positions and needs. Identifies roles and resources. Facilitates understanding and conflicting positions. Generates and facilitates generation of possible solutions. Gains cooperation or support when working with others.

Builds and maintains alliances	Establishes contact and interacts with others who share common interest, such as development, reaching goals, and giving advice. Maintains friendships, business associations, interest groups, and support networks. Influences perception about the organization. Understands the values of and learns from partnerships, associations, and other cooperative alliances.

LEADS BY EXAMPLE Leaders constantly serve as role models for others. Leaders will always be viewed as the example, so they must maintain standards and provide examples of effectiveness through all their actions. All Army leaders should model the Army Values. Modeling provides tangible evidence of desired behaviors and reinforces verbal guidance through demonstrations of commitment and action.	
Displays character by modeling the Army Values consistently through action, attitudes, and communication	Sets the example by displaying high standards of duty performance, personal appearance, military and professional bearing, physical fitness and health, and ethics. Fosters an ethical climate. Shows good moral judgment and behavior. Completes individual and unit tasks to standard, on time, and within the commander's intent. Is punctual and meets deadlines. Demonstrates determination, persistence, and patience.

Exemplifies the Warrior Ethos	Removes or fights through obstacles, difficulties, and hardships to accomplish the mission. Demonstrates the will to succeed. Demonstrates physical and emotional courage. Communicates how the Warrior Ethos is demonstrated.
Demonstrates commitment to Nation, Army, unit, Soldiers, community, and multinational partners	Demonstrates enthusiasm for task completion and, if necessary, methods of accomplishing assigned tasks. Is available to assist peers and subordinates. Shares hardships with subordinates. Participates in team tasks and missions without being asked.
Leads with confidence in adverse situations	Provides leader presence at the right time and place. Displays self-control, composure, and positive attitude, especially under adverse conditions. Is resilient. Remains decisive after discovering a mistake. Acts in the absence of guidance. Does not show discouragement when facing setbacks. Remains positive when the situation becomes confusing or changes. Encourages subordinates when they show signs of weakness.

Demonstrates technical and tactical knowledge and skills	Meets mission standards, protects resources, and accomplishes the mission with available resources using technical and tactical skills. Displays appropriate knowledge of equipment, procedures, and methods.
Understand the importance of conceptual skills and models them to others	Displays comfort working in open systems. Makes logical assumptions in the absence of facts. Identifies critical issues to use as a guide in making decisions and taking advantage of opportunities. Recognizes and generates innovative solutions. Relates and compares information from different sources to identify possible cause-and-effect relationships. Uses sound judgment and logical reasoning.
Seeks and is open to diverse ideas and points of view	Encourages respectful, honest communication among staff and decision makers. Explores alternative explanations and approaches for accomplishing tasks. Reinforces new ideas, demonstrates willingness to consider alternative perspectives to resolve difficult problems. Uses knowledgeable sources and subject matter experts. Recognizes and discourages individuals seeking to gain favor from tacit agreements.

<table>
<tr><th colspan="2">COMMUNICATES
Leaders communicate effectively by clearly expressing ideas and actively listening to others. By understanding the nature and importance of communication and practicing effective communication techniques, leaders will relate better to others and be able to translate goals into actions. Communication is essential to all other leadership competencies.</th></tr>
<tr><td>Listens actively</td><td>Listens and watches attentively.
Makes appropriate notes.
Tunes into content, emotion, and urgency.
Uses verbal and nonverbal means to reinforce to the speaker that you are paying attention.
Reflects on new information before expressing views.</td></tr>
<tr><td>Determines information-sharing strategies</td><td>Shares necessary information with others and subordinates.
Protects confidential information.
Coordinates plans with higher, lower, and adjacent individuals and attached organizations.
Keeps higher and lower headquarters, superiors, and subordinates informed.</td></tr>
<tr><td>Employs engaging communication techniques</td><td>States goals to energize others to adopt and act on them.
Speaks enthusiastically and maintains listeners' interest and involvement.
Makes appropriate eye contact when speaking.
Uses gestures that are appropriate but not distracting.
Uses visual aids as needed.
Acts to determine, recognize, and resolve misunderstandings.</td></tr>
</table>

Conveys thoughts and ideas to ensure shared understanding	Expresses thoughts and ideas clearly to individual groups. Uses correct grammar and doctrinally correct phrases. Recognizes potential miscommunication. Uses appropriate means for communicating a message. Communicates clearly and concisely up, down, across, and outside the organization. Clarifies when there is some question about goals, tasks, plans, performance expectations, and role responsibilities.
Presents recommendations so others understand advantages	Uses logic and relevant facts in dialogue. Keeps conversations on track. Expresses well-thought out and well-organized ideas.
Is sensitive to culture factors in communication	Maintains awareness of communication customs, expressions, actions, or behaviors. Demonstrates respect for others.

CREATES A POSITIVE ENVIRONMENT	
Leaders have the responsibility to establish and maintain positive expectations and attitudes that produce the setting for healthy relationships and effective work behaviors. Leaders are charged with improving the organization while accomplishing missions. They should leave the organization better than it was when they arrived.	
Fosters teamwork, cohesion, cooperation, and loyalty	Encourages people to work together effectively. Promotes teamwork and team achievement to build trust. Draws attention to the consequence of poor coordination. Acknowledges and rewards successful team coordination. Integrates new members into the unit quickly.
Encourages subordinates to exercise initiative, accept responsibility, and take ownership	Involves others in decisions and keeps them informed of consequences that affect them. Allocates responsibility for performance. Guides subordinate leaders in thinking through problems for themselves. Allocates decision making to the lowest appropriate level. Acts to expand and enhance subordinate's competence and self-confidence. Rewards initiative.

Creates a learning environment	Uses effective assessment and training methods. Encourages leaders and their subordinates to reach their full potential. Motives others to develop themselves. Expresses the value of interacting with others and seeking counsel. Stimulates innovative and critical thinking in others. Seeks new approaches to problems.
Encourages open and candid communication	Shows others how to accomplish tasks while remaining respectful, resolute, and focused. Communicates a positive attitude to encourage others and improve morale. Reinforces the expression of contrary and minority viewpoints. Displays appropriate reactions to new or conflicting information of opinions. Guards against group-think.
Encourages fairness and inclusiveness	Provides accurate evaluations and assessments. Supports equal opportunity. Prevents all forms of harassment. Encourages learning about and leveraging diversity.

Expresses and demonstrates care for people and their well-being	Encourages subordinates and peers to express candid opinions. Ensures that subordinates and their families are provided for, including their health, welfare, and development. Stands up for subordinates. Routinely monitors morale and encourages honest feedback.
Anticipates people's on-the-job needs	Recognizes and monitors subordinate's needs and reactions. Shows concern for the impact of tasks and missions on subordinate morale.
Sets and maintains high expectations for individuals and teams	Clearly articulates expectations. Creates a climate that expects good performances, recognizes superior performances, and does not accept poor performance. Challenges others to match the leader's example.
Accepts reasonable setbacks and failures	Communicates the difference between maintaining professional standards and a zero-defects mentality. Expresses the importance of being competent and motivated but recognizes the occurrence of failure. Emphasizes learning from one's mistakes.

PREPARES SELF	
Leaders ensure they are prepared to execute their leadership responsibilities fully. They are aware of their limitation and strengths and seek to develop themselves. Leaders maintain physical fitness and mental wellbeing. They continue to improve the domain knowledge required of their leadership roles and their profession. Only through continuous preparation for missions and other challenges, being aware of self and situation, and practicing lifelong learning and development can an individual fulfill the responsibilities of leadership.	
Maintains mental and physical health and well-being	Recognizes imbalance of inappropriateness of one's own actions. Removes emotions from decision making. Applies logic and reason to make decisions or when interacting with emotionally charged individuals. Recognizes the sources of stress and maintains appropriate levels of challenge to motivate self. Takes part in regular exercise, leisure activities, and time away from routine work. Stays focused on life priorities and values.

Maintains self awareness, employs self understanding, and recognizes impact on others	Evaluates one's strengths and weaknesses. Learns from mistakes and makes corrections, learns from experience. Considers feedback on performance, outcomes associated with actions, and actions taken by others to achieve similar goals. Seeks feedback on how others view one's own actions. Routinely determines personal goals and makes progress towards them. Develops capabilities where possible but accepts personal limitations. Seeks opportunities where capabilities can be used appropriately. Understands self-motivation under various tasks conditions.
Evaluates and incorporates feedback from others	Determines areas in need of development. Judges self with the help of feedback from others.
Expands knowledge of technical, technological, and tactical areas	Keeps informed about developments and policy changes inside and outside the organization. Seeks knowledge of systems, equipment, capabilities, and situations, particularly information technology systems.

Expands conceptual and interpersonal capabilities	Understands the contribution of concentration, critical thinking (assimilation of information, discriminating relevant cues, questions asking), imagination (decentering), and problem solving in different task conditions. Learns new approaches to problem solving. Applies lessons learned. Filters unnecessary information efficiently. Reserves time for self-development, reflection, and personal growth. Considers possible motives behind conflicting information.
Analyzes and organizes information to create knowledge	Reflects on what has been learned and organizes these insights for future application. Considers source, quality or relevance, and criticalness of information to improve understanding. Identifies reliable sources of data and other resources related to acquiring knowledge. Sets up systems of procedures to store knowledge for reuse.
Maintains relevant cultural awareness	Learns about issues of language, values, customary behavior, ideas, beliefs, and patterns of thinking that influence others. Learns about results of previous encounters when culture plays a role in mission success.

Maintains relevant geopolitical awareness	Learns about relevant societies outside the United States experiencing unrest. Recognizes Army influences on other countries, multinational partners, and enemies. Understands the factors influencing conflict and peacekeeping, peace enforcing, and peacemaking missions.

DEVELOPS OTHERS Leaders encourage and support others to grow as individuals and as a team. They facilitate the achievement of organizational goals through assisting others to develop. They prepare others to assume new positions elsewhere in the organization, making the organization more versatile and productive.	
Assesses current developmental needs of others	Observes and monitors subordinates under different task conditions to establish strengths and weaknesses. Notes changes in proficiency. Evaluates subordinates in a fair and consistent manner.
Fosters job development, job challenge, and job enrichment	Assessment tasks and subordinate motivation to consider methods of improving work assignments, when job enrichment would be useful, methods of cross-training on tasks, and methods of accomplishing missions. Designs tasks to provide practice in areas of subordinate's weaknesses. Designs ways to challenge subordinates and improve practice. Encourages subordinates to improve processes.

Counsels, coaches, and mentors	Improves subordinate's understanding and proficiency. Uses experiences and knowledge to improve future performances. Counsels, coaches, and mentors subordinates, subordinates leaders, and others.
Facilitates ongoing development	Maintains awareness of existing individuals and organizational development programs and removes barriers to development. Supports opportunities for self-development. Arranges training opportunities as needed that help subordinates improve self-awareness, confidence, and competence.
Supports institutional-based development	Encourages subordinates to pursue institutional learning opportunities. Provides information about institutional training and career progression to subordinates. Maintains resources related to development.
Builds team or group skills and processes	Presents challenging assignments for team or group interaction. Provides resources and support. Sustains and improves the relationships among team or groups members. Provides realistic, mission-oriented training. Provides feedback on team processes.

GETS RESULTS A leader's ultimate purpose is to accomplish organizational results. A leader gets results by providing guidance and managing resources, as well as performing the other leader competencies. This competency is focused on consistent and ethical tack accomplishment through supervising, managing, monitoring, and controlling of the work.	
Prioritizes, organizes, and coordinates tasking for teams or other organizational structures/groups	Uses planning to ensure each course of action to achieve the desired outcome. Organizes groups and teams to accomplish work. Plans to ensure that all tasks can be executed in the time available and that tasks depending on other tasks are executed in the correct sequence. Limits over specification and micromanagement.
Identifies and accounts for individual and group capabilities and commitment to task	Considers duty position, capabilities, and developmental needs when assigning tasks. Conducts initial assessments when beginning a new task or assuming a new position.
Designates, clarifies, and deconflicts roles	Establishes and employs procedures for monitoring, coordinating, and regulating subordinate's action and activities. Mediates peer conflicts and disagreements.

Identifies, contends for, allocates, and manages recourses	Allocates adequate time for task completion. Keeps tracks of people and equipment. Allocates time to prepare and conduct rehearsals. Continually seeks improvement in operating efficiency, resource conservation, and fiscal responsibility. Attracts, recognizes, and retains talent.
Removes work barriers	Protects organizations from unnecessary tasking and distractions. Recognizes and resolves scheduling conflicts. Overcomes other obstacles preventing full attention to accomplishing the mission.
Recognizes and rewards good performance	Recognizes individual and team accomplishments; rewards them appropriately. Credits subordinates for good performance. Builds on successes. Explores new reward systems and understands individual reward motivations.

Seeks, recognizes, and takes advantage of opportunities to improve performance	Asks incisive questions. Anticipates needs for action. Analyzes activities to determine how the desired end is achieved or effected. Acts to improve the organization's collective performance. Envisions ways to improve. Recommends best methods for accomplishing tasks. Leverages information and communication technology to improve individual and group effectiveness. Encourages staff to use creativity to solve problems.
Makes feedback part of work processes	Gives and seeks accurate and timely feedback. Uses feedback to modify duties, tasks, procedures, requirements, and goals when appropriate. Uses assessment techniques and evaluation tools (such as AARs) to identify lessons learned and facilitate consistent improvement. Determines the appropriate setting and timing for feedback.

Executes plans to accomplish the mission	Schedules activities to meet all commitments in critical performance areas. Notifies peers and subordinates in advance when their support is required. Keeps track of task assignments and suspense's. Adjusts assignments, if necessary. Attends to details.
Identifics and adjusts to external influences on the mission or tasking and organizations	Gathers and analyzes relevant information about changing situations. Determines causes, effects and contributing factors of problems. Considers contingencies and their consequences. Makes necessary, on-the-spot adjustments.

ATTRIBUTES **A Leader of Character** (Identity) Factors internal and central to a leader, that which makes up an individual's core.	
Army Values	Values are the principles, standards, or qualities considered essential for successful leaders. Values are fundamentals to help people discern right from wrong in any situation. The Army has set seven values that must be developed in all Army individuals: loyalty, duty, respect, selfless service, honor, integrity, and personal courage.

Empathy	The propensity to experience something from another person's point of view. The ability to identify with and enter into another person's feelings and emotions. The desire to care for and take care of soldiers and others.
Warrior Ethos	The shared sentiment internal to soldiers that represents the spirit of the profession of arms.

A LEADER WITH PRESENCE How a leader is perceived by others based on the leader's outward appearance, demeanor, actions, and words.	
Military Bearing	Possessing a commanding presence. Projecting a professional image of authority.
Physically fit	Having sound health, strength, and endurance that support one's emotional health and conceptual abilities under prolonged stress.
Confident	Projecting self-confidence and certainty in the unit's ability to succeed in whatever it does. Demonstrating composure and an outward calm through steady control over one's emotions.
Resilient	Showing a tendency to recover quickly from setbacks, shocks, injuries, adversity, and stress while maintaining a mission and organizational focus.

A LEADER WITH INTELLECTUAL CAPACITY The mental resources or tendencies that shape a leader's conceptual abilities and impact of effectiveness.	
Agility	Flexibility of mind. Tendency to anticipate or adapt to uncertain or changing situation; to think through second-and third-order effects when current decisions or actions are not producing the desired effects. The ability to break out of mental "sets" or habitual thought patterns: to improvise when faced with conceptual impasses. The ability to quickly apply multiple perspectives and approaches to assessment, conceptual impasses. The ability to quickly apply multiple perspectives and approaches to assessment, conceptualization, and evaluation.
Judgment	The capacity to assess situations or circumstances shrewdly and to draw sound conclusions. The tendency to form sound opinions and make sensible decisions and reliable guesses. The ability to make sound decisions when all facts are not available.
Innovative	The tendency to introduce new ideas when opportunity exists in the face of challenging circumstances. Creativity in the production of ideas and objects that are both novel or original and worthwhile or appropriate.

Interpersonal tact	The capacity to understand interactions with others. Being aware of how others see you and sensing how to interact with them effectively. Consciousness of character and motives of others and how that affects interacting with them.
Domain knowledge	Possessing facts, beliefs, and logical assumptions in relevant areas. Technical knowledge—specialized information associated with a particular function or system. Tactical knowledge—understanding military tactics related to securing a designated objective through military means. Joint knowledge—understanding joint organizations, their procedures, and their roles in national defense. Cultural and geopolitical knowledge—understanding cultural, geographic, and political differences and sensitivities.

TAC Staff will use the FM 6-22 as their guide while rating candidates (you). Be a positive influence on your fellow candidates while in leadership, or plan on packing your bags.

Chapter 8

Schedule Breakdown

"Criticism should not be querulous and wasting,
but guiding, instructive, inspiring."

— Ralph Waldo Emerson

**Note: This is a general schedule. Specific training schedules will be provided by OCS regiment upon entry into the program.*

FEDERAL OCS

Week 1: In-processing and Orientation

This week introduces you to the standards, procedures, and regulations under which you will live for the next 12 weeks. Attention to detail is stressed, as is efficient management of time.

Training: Initial APFT, Obstacle Course, Combat Water Survival Test, Map Reading.
References: The Constitution, FM 22-100, Familiarization with OCS SOP

Week 2: WTBD's (Warrior Tasks and Battle Drills)

This week introduces you to Warrior Tasks and Battle Drills. The priority is to train and execute selected individual warrior tasks in a field environment. All training uses the crawl / walk / run methodology. All training is conducted to familiarize / prepare you for

Field Leadership Exercises and ultimately to be a future leader in the Army.

Training: Call for Fire, 5-Mile Foot March
References: FM 7-8, TRADOC PAM 600-4, Familiarization with OCS SOP

Week 3: Leadership

This week introduces the core dimensions of Army BE-KNOW-DO leadership doctrine and describes the importance of competent and confident leadership to successful Army operations across the entire spectrum of conflict. It provides the doctrinal foundation for all subsequent periods of instruction on the direct leadership actions of influencing, operating, and improving that will be discussed in subsequent periods of the leadership blocks of instruction.

Training: Leadership Classes, 3-Mile Release Run, Leader's Reaction Course
References: FM 6-22, TRADOC PAM 600-4, Familiarize self with OCS SOP

Week 4: Tactics and Operations

This week introduces you to the characteristics of the offense, and the principles and characteristics of the defense. You will apply what you learn from classroom instruction to implement Troop Leading Procedures (TLPs).

Training: Troop Leading Procedures, 7-Mile Foot March, 4-Mile Release Run
References: Read FM 7-8, FM 3-0, Familiarize self with OCS SOP

Week 5: OPORD's and Training Management

This week introduces you to the Operations Order (OPORD). It also provides an overview of the training management system, which includes the training mission and principles of training. Battle-focused training, mission essential task list development, and after-action reviews are also focused on during this week.

Training: Operations Order, Reading and Writing in the Army Style
References: Read FM 7-8, FM 7-1

Week 6: History 1 and Branching

As an OCS Candidate, you must understand the utility of military history in today's Army and the major events in the military history of the United States from its colonial settlement through the Civil War. This week consists of instruction in this area.

Training: Prep for Deployment

Week 7: Field Leadership Exercise 1

During this week you will be introduced to leadership skills you will need in a field environment. You will also be introduced to the tactics, techniques, and procedures (TTP) required in order to navigate from one point to another and given practical work on tasks taught and applied during map reading.

Training: Senior Officer Candidate Review, 7-Mile Foot March, Land Navigation

Week 8: Field Leadership Exercise 2, SQD Squad Training Exercise (STX)

This week you will be instructed in and evaluated on selected individual and collective tasks in the operation of a squad.

Training: Field Exercise
References: FM 6-22

Week 9: Field Leadership Exercise 2, PLT Platoon Training Exercise (STX)

This week you will be instructed in and evaluated on selected individual and collective tasks in the operation of a platoon.

Training: Field Exercise, 10-Mile Foot March

Week 10: Recovery, History 2

This week you will learn to recover a unit from deployment and gain an understanding of the causes, strategies, events, and results of major combat and peacekeeping operations from WWI to the present.

Training: Graduation Run, Battalion Commander Social

Week 11: Officership

This week provides you with the opportunity to explore leadership topics with senior officers who have experienced the same or similar situations. Topics include counseling, reception and integration, career advice, NCO-Officer relationship, and other subjects chosen by candidates.

Training: Final APFT, Company 5-Mile Run

Week 12: Graduation

You will take the oath of office and complete final preparation for graduation.

Training: Commissioning Oath, Graduation

STATE OCS

Listed below is the State Fast Track schedule. Weeks 3 through 7 are executed during traditional OCS drill weekends over a 12-month period.

Week 1: Introduction

This week introduces you to the standards, procedures, and regulations under which you will live for the next eight weeks. TACs enforce a very stressful atmosphere at all times.

Training: Initial APFT, Map Reading, Land Navigation
References: FM 22-100, Familiarize self with OCS SOP

Week 2: Land Navigation

The stress level remains very high. You will go into the field to perform day and night land navigation instruction. Candidates who do not pass are given one additional opportunity to earn a "GO." Those who do not pass after a second attempt will be sent home.

Training: Map Reading, Land Navigation
References: FM 7-8, Familiarize self with OCS SOP

Week 3: Leadership

This week introduces you to the core dimensions of what was formerly Army BE-KNOW-DO leadership doctrine and describes the importance of competent/confident leadership to successful Army operations across the entire spectrum of conflict. It provides the doctrinal foundation for all subsequent periods of instruction on the direct leadership actions of influencing, operating, and improving that will also be discussed in subsequent periods of the leadership blocks of instruction.

Training: Leadership Classes, 3-Mile Release Run, Leader's Reaction Course
References: FM 6-22, TRADOC PAM 600-4, Familiarize self with OCS SOP

Week 4: Tactics and Operations

This week will introduce you to the characteristics of the offense and the principles and characteristics of the defense. You will also apply classroom instruction theory to implement Troop Leading Procedures (TLPs).

Training: Troop Leading Procedures, 7-Mile Foot March, 4-Mile Release Run
References: Read FM 7-8, FM 3-0, Familiarize self with OCS SOP

Week 5: OPORD's and Training Management

This week introduces you to the Operations Order (OPORD). It also provides you with an overview of the training management system that includes the training mission and the principles of training. Battle-focused training, mission essential task list development, and after-action reviews are also focused on during this week.

Training: Operations Order, Reading and Writing in the Army Style
References: Read FM 7-8, FM 7-1

Week 6: History 1 and Branching

As an OCS Candidate, you must understand the utility of military history in today's Army and the major events in the military history of the United States from its colonial settlement through the Civil War. This week consists of instruction in this area.

Training: Prep for Deployment

Week 7: Field Leadership Exercise 1

This week you will be introduced to leadership skills you will need in a field environment. You will also be introduced to the tactics, techniques, and procedures required to navigate from one point to another and given practical work on tasks taught during applied map reading.

Training: Senior Officer Candidate Review, 7-Mile Foot March, Land Navigation

Week 8: Field Leadership Exercise 2, Squad Training Exercise (STX)

This week you will be instructed in and evaluated on selected individual and collective tasks in the operation of a squad.

Training: Field Exercise
References: FM 6-22

Week 9: Field Leadership Exercise 2, PLT STX

This week you will be instructed in and evaluated on selected individual and collective tasks in the operation of a platoon.

Training: Field Exercise, 10-Mile Foot March, Obstacle Course, Combat Water Survival Test WTBDs (Warrior Tasks and Battle Drills).

Chapter 9

Troop Leading Procedures

"Luck is where preparation meets opportunity."

— Sterling W. Sill

TROOP LEADING PROCEDURES

a) Receive the Mission

1) Conduct a Confirmation Brief to understand:

a) Commander's intent

b) Specific tasks and purposes

c) The relationship of tasks to those of other elements conducting the operation

d) The important coordinating measures

b) Issue a Warning Order

c) Make a Tentative Plan

d) Start Necessary Movement

e) Reconnoiter (5 point contingency plan or GOTWA)

1) Where the leader is Going

2) Others going with the leader

3) Amount of Time the leader plans to be gone

4) What to do if the leader does not return

5) Unit's and leader's Actions on chance contact while the leader is gone

f) Complete the Plan

g) Issue the Complete Order

h) Supervise: The best plan may fail if it is not managed right. Rehearsals (five types: confirmation brief, back brief, combined arms, support, and battle drill or SOP), inspections, and continuous coordination of plans must be used to supervise and refine troop-leading procedures.

1) Confirmation briefs and back briefs are used to ensure that all subordinates understand the operation completely (see TLP, Para A, Receive the Mission) and review to the commander how they intend to accomplish the mission (back brief).

2) All other rehearsals: focus on mission execution.

a) They are essential to ensure complete coordination and subordinate understanding.
b) The warning order should provide subordinate leaders with sufficient level of detail for them to schedule and conduct rehearsals of drills/SOPs before receiving the OPORD.
c) Rehearsals conducted after the OPORD can then focus on mission specific tasks.
d) Rehearsals should be conducted in a training area as much like the objective as possible.
e) Mock-ups of the objective should be used for these practices.
f) Rehearsals include holding soldier and leader back briefs of individual tasks and using sand tables or sketches to talk through the execution of the plan.
g) These are followed by walk through exercises and then full speed blank-fire or live-fire rehearsals.
h) The leader should establish a priority for rehearsals based on available time. The priority of rehearsals flows from the decisive point of the operation. Thus the order of precedence is:
1) actions on the objective
2) battle drills for maneuver

3) actions on enemy contact
4) special teams
5) movement techniques
6) others as required
i) Security must be maintained during the rehearsal.

3) Inspections:
a) Squad leaders should conduct initial inspections shortly after receipt of the WARNO
b) The PSG should conduct spot checks throughout the preparation
c) The PL and PSG conduct final inspections
d) Inspections should include:
1) Weapons and ammunition
2) Uniforms and equipment
3) Mission-essential equipment
4) Soldier's understanding of the mission and their specific responsibilities
5) Communications
6) Rations and water
7) Camouflage
8) Deficiencies noted during earlier inspections

Chapter 10

Orders

"Plan your work, and work your plan."

—Norman Vincent Peale

1. Orders Group

A. Platoon orders: at a minimum, the following individuals will attend platoon orders:

1) Platoon leader
2) Platoon sergeant
3) Squad leaders
4) Platoon FO
5) PLT Medic
6) Attachment leaders

B. Squad orders: at a minimum, the following individuals will attend squad:

1) Squad leader
2) Team leaders

2. Orders Formats

A. Warning order (WARNO)

1) Situation
2) Mission
3) Execution

a) Concept
b) Time Schedule
c) Rehearsal
d) Tasks to Subordinates
4) Service Support
5) Command and Signal

B. Fragmentary order (FRAGO): The format for a FRAGO is that portion of the current OPORD that has changed. If significant changes have occurred since the last OPORD, a new OPORD should be prepared.

C. Squad Operation Order
1) Situation
a) Enemy
b) Friendly
c) Attachments and Detachments
2) Mission
a) Who, What, When, Where, Why
3) Execution
a) Concept of the Operation
1) Scheme of Maneuver
2) Fire Support
b) Fire Team Tasks
c) Coordinating Instructions
d) Safety
4) Service Support
5) Command and Signal

D. Platoon Operation Order
1) Situation
a) Enemy Forces
1) Disposition, composition, and strength
2) Capabilities
3) Most probable course of action
b) Friendly Forces
1) Higher Unit

2) Left Unit's Mission
3) Right Unit's Mission
4) Forward Unit's Mission
5) Mission of Unit in Reserve or Following
6) Units in Support or Reinforcing Higher Unit

c) Attachments and Detachments

2) Mission Task and Purpose (Who, What, When, Where, Why)

3) Execution: Intent (Expanded Purpose: Key Tasks: Endstate)

a) Concept of the Operation: How unit accomplishes the mission.

1) Maneuver: Designate main effort and ID tasks

2) Fires: Concept of fire support, address priority of fires, priority targets, and restrictive control measures

3) Additional combat support elements: Concept of employment and priority of effort

b) Tasks to Maneuver Units: Tasks and purpose for each

c) Tasks to combat support units

d) Coordinating Instructions

1) Priority intelligence requirements and report tasks
2) MOPP level (Mission-oriented protective posture)
3) Troop safety and operational exposure guide
4) Engagement and disengagement criteria and instructions
5) Fire distribution and control measures
6) Consolidation and reorganization instructions
7) Reporting requirements
8) Specified tasks that pertain to more than one task
9) Rules of engagement
10) Order of march and other movement procedures

e) Safety

4) Service Support

a) General: Provide training location, Casualty and damaged equipment collection points, and routes to and from them.

b) Material and services

1) Supply

a) Class I: Subsistence
b) Class II: Clothing, ind. equip., tools, and tent packages
c) Class III: Petroleum, oil, and lubricants
d) Class IV: Construction materials

e) Class V: Ammunition
f) Class VI: Personal demand items
g) Class VII: Major end items
h) Class VIII: Medical supplies
i) Class IX: Repair parts
2) Transportation: Schedule and distribution
3) Services: Type, designation, location.
4) Maintenance
5) Medical evacuation (See Appendix F)
a) Personnel: EPW collection point and handling instructions.
b) Miscellaneous
5) Command and Signal
a) Command
1) Location of higher unit commander and Command Post (CP)
2) Location of unit leader or CP
3) Location of second in command or alternate CP
4) Succession of command: During combat, any member of the platoon may be required to assume command. Frequently, the platoon FO or RATELO may need to continue operations and direct the operation until the chain of command can be reestablished. Under normal conditions, the platoon succession of command will be:
a) Platoon leader
b) Platoon sergeant
c) Main effort squad leader
d) Supporting effort squad leaders by rank
b) Signal
1) SOI index in effect
2) Listening silence if applicable
3) Methods of communication in priority
4) Emergency signals
5) Code words

Chapter 11

Success During Squad Lanes

"I was too weak to defend, so I attacked."

— Robert E. Lee after his victory at Chancellorsville

One of the final rating periods you will undergo during OCS is Squad Training Lanes. All candidates will go to the field as a company and then break down to squad level for missions. The squad leader is rated using the Field Leadership Evaluation Report (FLER). Typically, each squad is assigned six missions per day. Each mission takes about two hours from the time the mission is received through the after-action review (AAR). The STX mission typically goes like this:

Candidate Receives mission: Lane guide or TAC will read platoon OPORD to Squad Leader. Candidate initiates eight Troop Leading Procedures (TLPs)

Plan: The plan is created and OPORD is briefed on the candidate-made sand table. (See next paragraph.)

Cross Line of Departure (LD): Once the squad OPORD is given and rehearsals are complete, the SL request permission to cross the LD.

Execution of Mission: Missions vary from movement to contact to an area recon. Depending on the lane and what the lane guide or TAC think, a FRAGO might be issued for an alternative mission. This requires Squad Leaders to think on the move and reorganize their squad to complete the alternate mission.

AAR: Once the smoke settles and the mission is complete, each squad performs an after-action review of the mission. It is typical for Squad Leaders to lead the review by restating the mission statement and then talking through what actually happened on the lane. Finally, the squad members offer three sustains (acts performed by soldiers) and three improves (acts that need improvement) for the rated candidate. The next rated candidate prepares for the next mission by selecting the team leaders who will lead it.

Evaluation: The TAC will pull you aside to provide evaluation results as the squad moves to the next lane starting point with the lane guide. Leadership performance ratings range from N to E:

N: Needs improvement. You did not meet the requirements.
S: Satisfactory. You met the requirements.
E: Excellent. You exceeded the requirements.

In order to pass, you must earn at least an "S" during the rated squad lane. Proper execution of the troop leading procedure prior to crossing the line of departure is weighted heavily. However, if you execute the TLPs but freeze during the execution of the mission, you may still earn an "N" rating.

Terrain Model Kit

You need to purchase alcohol markers for use during STX lanes. You can get these from most surplus stores or online at Ranger Joes or US Patriot. Be sure you purchase the alcohol eraser pen with the markers. They are sometimes sold individually.

Keep a good stash of yarn for phase lines on the sand table. Bring extra for your fellow candidates to utilize.

Pull out the terrain model kit in Appendix G, laminate the paper, and then cut the individual pieces out and secure them in a zip lock bag.

Other items for the terrain model kit include:

- 550 Cord (15 feet)
- White String or 550 Cord Guts (15 feet)
- Yarn : blue, green, and yellow (15 feet of each color)
- Alcohol pen set (both fine and medium point)
- Alcohol eraser pen or small bottle of alcohol

Sand Table

You must create a sand table quickly. Typically, when you receive your mission the Squad Leader will bring along a scribe. Always request that a scribe and a team leader are present for the mission brief. The worst that can happen is that you will be told "no." Whoever attends the mission brief with the Squad Leader sets up the sand table.

Keys to Building a Sand Table

- Be quick about it. It is not meant to be a masterpiece. Focus on key terrain features by using the terrain model kit for labeling.

- Set the terrain model up in the direction of travel. It will help minimize the likelihood of misunderstandings.

- Use phase lines to break down the mission. Brief it in phases to help minimize the likelihood of misunderstandings. Don't use more then four phases.

- Orient all squad members to the terrain model before you begin the OPORD. This will ensure that everyone is on the same page as soon as possible.

- Use a pointer and move the pieces while briefing the mission execution. Again, this will get every squad member on same page as soon as possible.

- Be sure to show actions on contact and security when moving the terrain model pieces on the sand table.

- Save time for rehearsals.

(See example of a Sand Table on the following page)

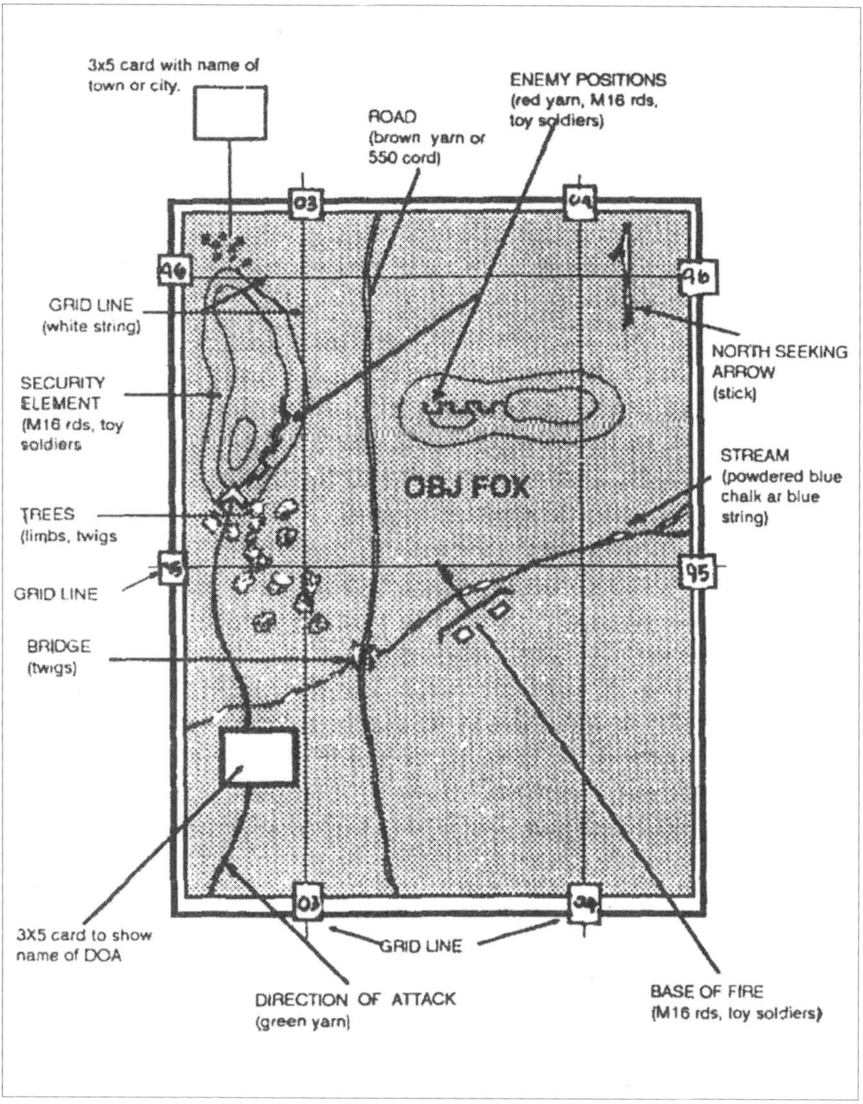

Sand Table

Movement Formations

Squad Leaders need to ensure their squad moves out in a tactical formation. "Gaggle File" (a "gaggle" is an unorganized group of soldiers) may or may not be an approved formation. Get it right, look sharp, and complete the mission with high motivation.

Formation: Leaders choose the formation based on their analysis of Mission Enemy Terrain Time Troops (METT-T) and the likelihood of enemy contact.

(1) *Fire Team Formations*: All soldiers in the team must be able to see their leader.

> (a) *Wedge*: This is the basic fire team formation. You will use it unless it is modified because of terrain, dense vegetation, or the mission.
>
> (b) *File*: This is used in close terrain, usually dense vegetation with limited visibility.

(2) *Squad Formations*: Squad formations describe the relationships between fire teams in the squad.

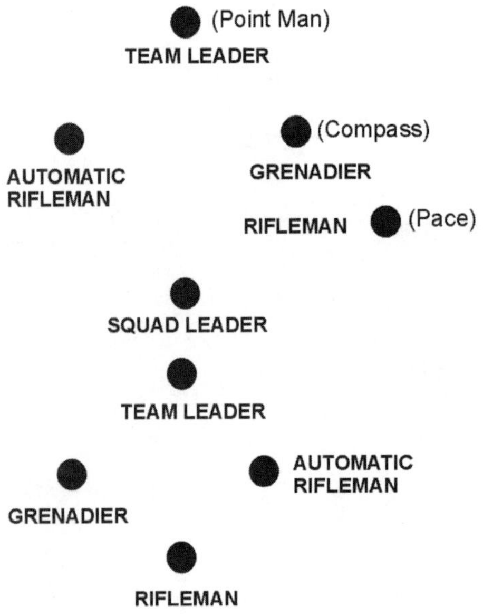

(a) *Column*:

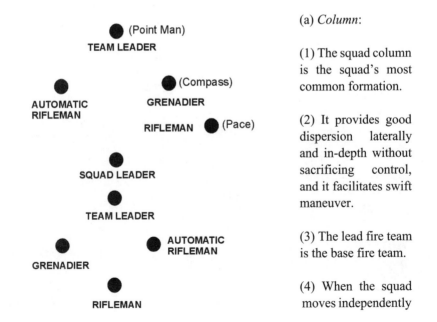

(1) The squad column is the squad's most common formation.

(2) It provides good dispersion laterally and in-depth without sacrificing control, and it facilitates swift maneuver.

(3) The lead fire team is the base fire team.

(4) When the squad moves independently

or as the rear element of the platoon, the rifleman in the trail fire team provides rear security.

(b) *Line*:

(1) The squad line provides maximum firepower to the front.

(2) When a squad is acting as the base squad, the fire team on the right is the base fire team.

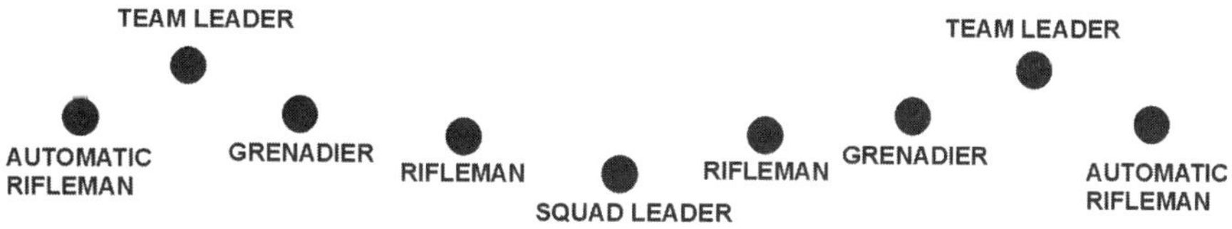

(c) *File*:

(1) When not traveling in a column or line, squads travel in file.

(2) The squad file has the same characteristics as the fire team file.

(3) If the Squad leader desires to increase his control over the formation, exert greater morale presence by leading from the front, and be available to make key decisions, he will move ahead to the first or second position.

(4) Additional control over the rear of the formation can be provided by moving a team leader to the last position.

Fire Control

Squad lanes are normally run prior to platoon and company lanes. These fire control measures are mostly for when you are setting up a perimeter with the intent to defend in place. These will prove to be very handy during STX and patrol lanes.

1. Fire Control Measures

(a) Graphic measures

(1) Boundaries or sectors
(2) Battle positions
(3) Engagement areas
(4) Target Reference Points (TRPs)
(5) Maximum engagement lines
(6) Trigger lines
(7) Phase lines
(8) Final protective fire

(b) Rules of engagement

(c) Engagement priorities

(d) Machine Guns

(1) Leaders position machine guns to . . .

(a) Concentrate fires where they want to kill the enemy

(b) Fire across the platoon front

(c) Cover obstacles by fire

(d) Tie-in with adjacent units

(2) The following definitions apply to the employment of machine guns.

(a) Grazing fire

(b) Dead space

(c) Final protective line

(d) Platoon machine guns have the following target priority:

(1)The FPF, if directed

(2) The most dangerous or threatening target

(3) Groups of dismounted infantry in primary sector

(4) Enemy crew-served weapons

(5) Groups of dismounted infantry in secondary sector

(6) Unarmored command and control vehicles

2. Fire Commands

(a) *Alert*: The leader can alert the soldiers by name or unit designation, by some type of visual or sound signal, by personal contact, or by any other practical way.

(b) *Direction*: The general direction or pinpoint location of the target.

(c) *Description*: Describes the target briefly but accurately

(d) *Range*: Range to the target in meters

(e) *Method of Fire*: Which weapons, type & amount of ammunition, and the rate of fire.

(f) *Command to Fire*

3. Fire Distribution: The two methods of fire distribution are point fire and area fire.

(a) Point Fire: The platoon's fires are directed at one target. The platoon leader accomplishes this by marking the desired target with tracer fire or by M203 file.

(b) Area Fire. The platoon's fires cover an area from left to right and in depth. The platoon leader accomplishes this four ways.

(1) Frontal fire
(2) Cross fire
(3) Depth fire
(4) Combination

Range Cards

Range Cards will need to be created by each firing position once soldiers are placed by the Platoon / Squad Leader. By following the steps provided, Range Cards should be to standard and a useful tool for leaders while planning operations.

(1) The marginal information at the top of the card is listed as follows:

(a) The squad (SQD), platoon (PLT), and company (CO) designations are listed. Units higher than company are not listed.

(b) MAGNETIC NORTH. The range card is oriented with the terrain and the direction of magnetic north arrow is drawn.

(2) The gunner's sector of fire is drawn in the sector sketch section. It is not drawn to scale, but the data referring to the targets must be accurate.

(a) The weapon symbol is drawn in the center of the small circle.

(b) Left and right limits are drawn from the position. A circled "L" and "R" are placed at the end of the appropriate limit lines.

(c) The value of each circle is determined by using a terrain feature farthest from the position that is within the weapon's capability. The distance to the terrain is determined and rounded off to the next even hundredth, if necessary. The maximum number of circles that will divide evenly into the distance is determined and divided. The result is the value for each circle. The terrain feature is then drawn on the appropriate circle.

(d) All target reference points (TRPs) and key terrain are drawn in the sector. They are numbered consecutively and circled.

(e) Dead space is drawn in the sector.

(f) A maximum engagement line is drawn on range cards for anti-armor weapons.

(g) The weapon reference point is numbered last. The location is given a six-digit grid coordinate. When there is no terrain feature to be designated, the location is shown as an 8-digit grid coordinate.

(3) The data section is filled in as follows:

(a) *Position Identification*: The position is identified as primary alternate, or supplementary.

(b) *Date*. The date and time the range card was completed is entered.
(c) *Weapon*. The weapon block indicates the weapons used.

(d) *Each Circle Equals* ______ *Meters*: Write in the distance in meters between circles.

(e) *NO*: Starting with left and right limits TRPs and reference points are listed in numerical order.

(f) *Direction/Deflection*: The direction is listed in degrees. The deflection is listed in mils.

(g) *Elevation*: The elevation is listed in mils.

(h) *Range*: The distance in meters from the position [to the left and right limits and TRPs and reference points.

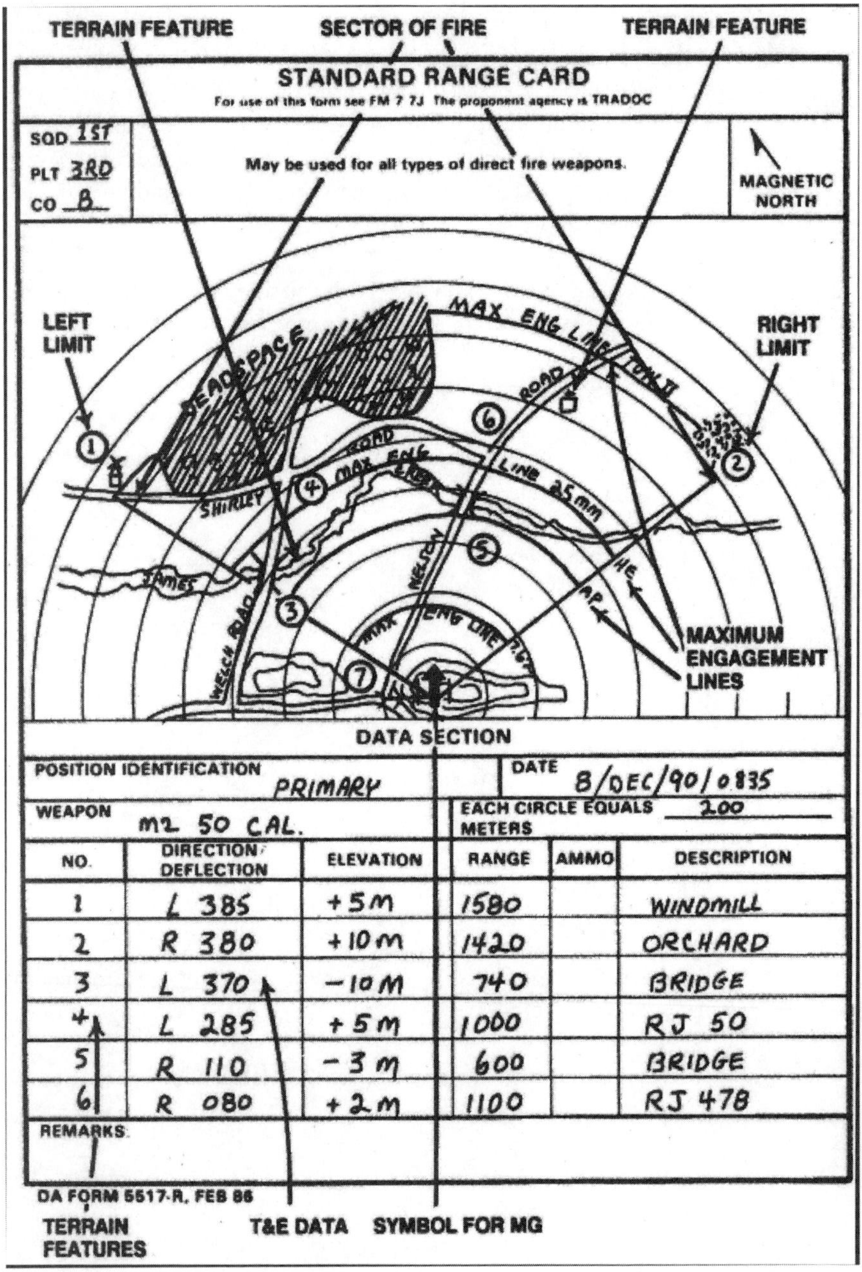

NO.	DIRECTION/ DEFLECTION	ELEVATION	RANGE	AMMO	DESCRIPTION
1	L 385	+5m	1580		WINDMILL
2	R 380	+10m	1420		ORCHARD
3	L 370	−10m	740		BRIDGE
4	L 285	+5m	1000		RJ 50
5	R 110	−3m	600		BRIDGE
6	R 080	+2m	1100		RJ 478

(i) *Ammo*: The type of ammunition used is listed.

(j) *Description*: The name of the object is listed for example, farmhouse, wood line, and hilltop.

(k) *Remarks*: The weapon reference point data and any additional information are listed.

Sector Sketches

Sector Sketches combine all individual rage cards into one overall snapshot of the unit's sector. If the range cards are not filled out properly, the Sector Sketch will be inaccurate and areas will be left unprotected. Always do it right from the lowest level up for success.

Squad

Squad Sector Sketches: Squad Leaders prepare an original and one copy of the Sector Sketch. The original remains in the squad command post, and the copy is turned in to the platoon leader. As a minimum, the squad Sector Sketch includes:

(1) Key terrain within the squad sector.
(2) Each individual fighting position and its primary and secondary sectors of fire.
(3) Key weapons positions and their primary sector of fire, secondary sector of fire, and any fire control measures.
(4) All CP and OP locations.
(5) All dead space within the squad sector.
(6) Any obstacles and mines within the squad sector.

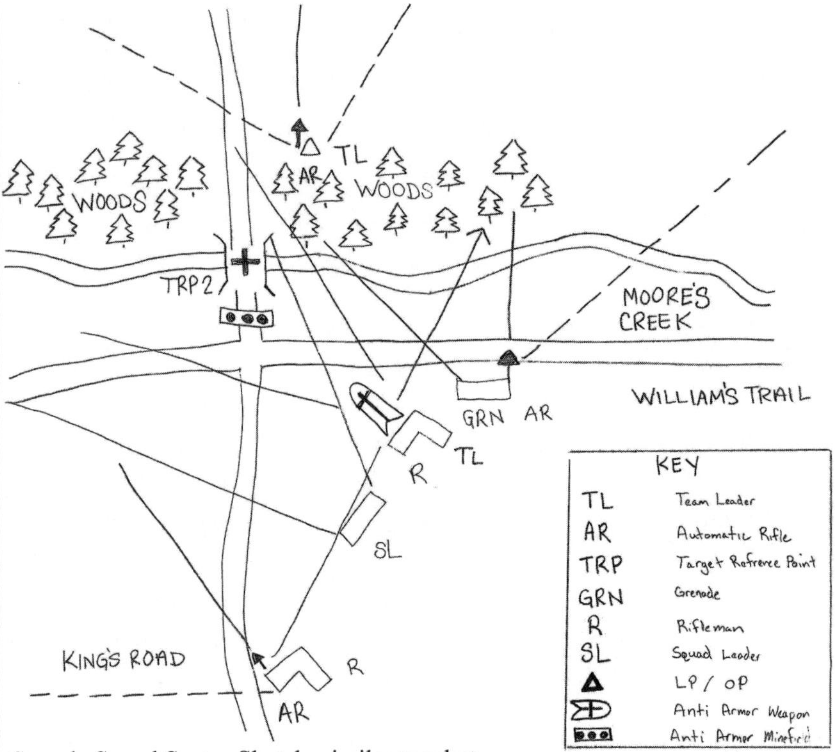

Sample Squad Sector Sketch, similar to what you will see and use in the field.

Platoon

Platoon Sector Sketches: Platoon leaders prepare an original and one copy of the Sector Sketch. The original remains in the platoon command post and the copy is turned in to the company commander. As a minimum, the platoon Sector Sketch includes:

(1) Squad positions and sectors of fire.
(2) Key weapons positions and their sectors of fire and fire control measures.
(3) CPs (Command Post), OPs (Observation Post), and patrol routes.
(4) Platoon maximum engagement lines.
(5) All dead space within the platoon sector.
(6) All mines and obstacles within the platoon sector.

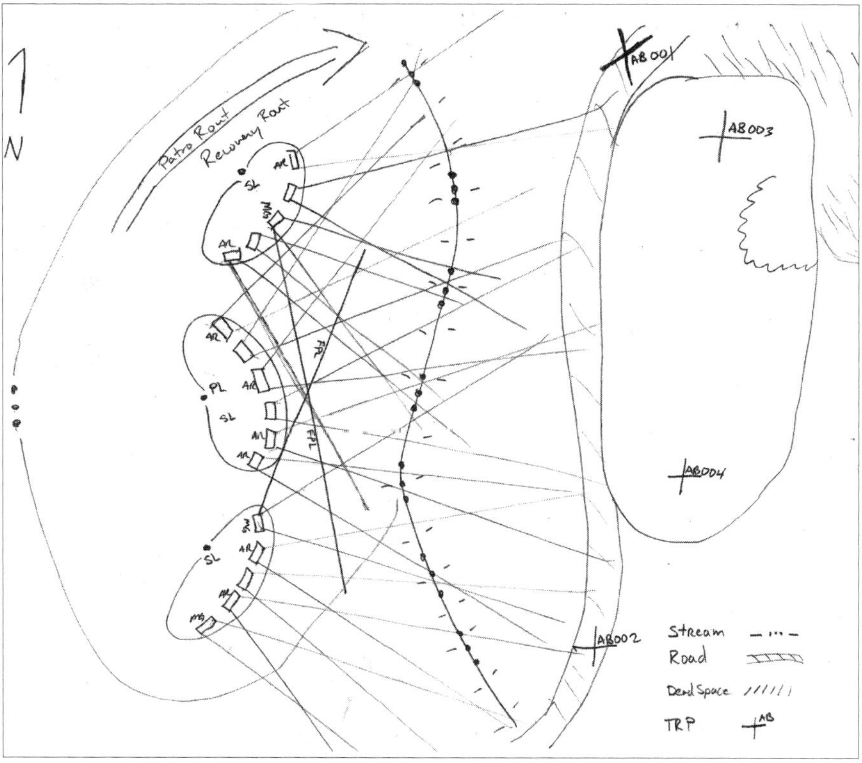

Sample Platoon Sector Sketch, similar to what you will see and use in the field.

(7) Any TRPs or FPFs (Final Protective Fires) within he platoon sector.

Hand and Arm Signals

ASSEMBLE or RALLY: Raise the arm vertically overhead, palm to the front, and wave in large, horizontal circles. NOTE: Signal is normally followed by the signaler pointing to the assembly or rally site.

JOIN ME, FOLLOW ME, or COME FORWARD: Point toward person(s) or unit(s); beckon by holding the arm horizontally to the front, palm up, and motioning toward the body.

INCREASE SPEED, DOUBLE TIME, or RUSH: Raise the fist to the shoulder; thrust the fist up-ward to the full extent of the arm and back to shoulder level, do this rapidly several times.

QUICK TIME: Extend the arm horizontally sideward, palm to the front, and wave the arm slightly downward several times, keeping the arm straight. Do not move the arm above the horizontal.

ENEMY IN SIGHT: Hold the rifle in the ready position at shoulder level. Point the rifle in the direction of the enemy.

TAKE COVER: Extend the arm at a 45-degree angle from the side, above the horizontal, palm down, and then lower the arm to the side.

WEDGE: Extend arms downward and to the sides at an angle of 45-degrees below the horizontal, palms to the front.

VEE: Raise the arms and extend them 45-degrees above the horizontal.

LINE: Extend the arms parallel to the ground.

ECHELON LEFT: Extend the right arm and raise it 45-degrees above the shoulder. Extend the left arm 45-degrees below the horizon and point toward the ground.

ECHELON RIGHT: Extend the left arm and raise it 45-degrees above the shoulder. Extend the right arm 45-degrees below the horizon and point toward the ground.

STAGGERED COLUMN: Extend the arms so that upper arms are parallel to the ground and the forearms are perpendicular. Raise the arms so they are fully extended above the head. Repeat.

COLUMN: Raise and extend the arm overhead. Move it to the right and left. Continue until the formation is executed.

TRAVELING OVERWATCH: Extend both arms and raise them up and down.

MOVE TO LEFT: Extend the arm to the left and raise it up and down.

MOVE TO RIGHT: Extend the arm to the right and raise it up and down.

CONTACT LEFT: Extend the left arm parallel to the ground. Bend the arm until the forearm is perpendicular. Repeat.

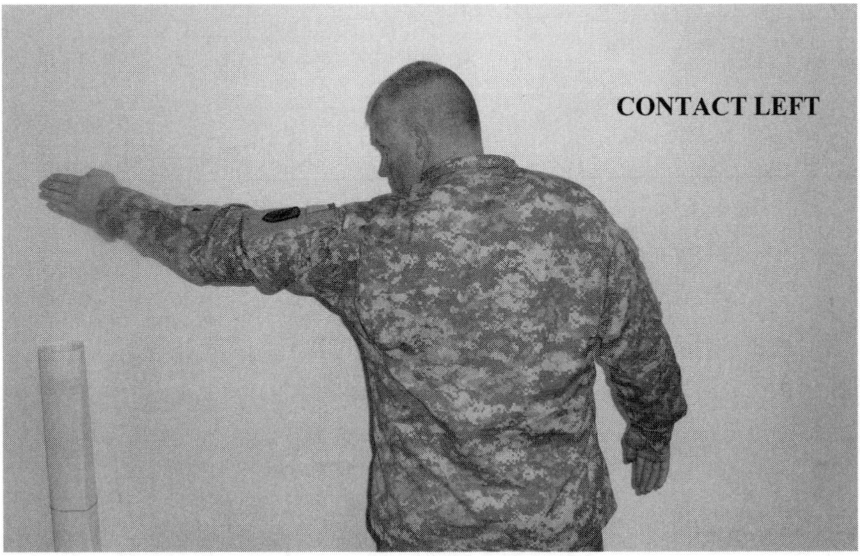

CONTACT RIGHT: Extend the right arm parallel to the ground. Bend the arm until the forearm is perpendicular. Repeat.

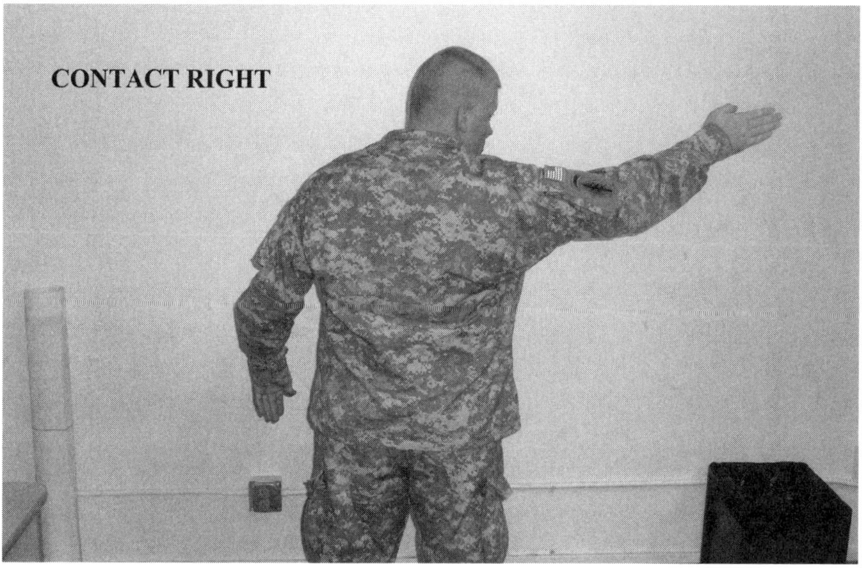

ACTION LEFT: Extend both arms parallel to the ground. Raise the right arm until it is overhead. Repeat.

ACTION RIGHT: Extend both arms parallel to the ground. Raise the left arm until it is overhead. Repeat.

MAP CHECK: Point at the palm of one hand with the Index finger of the other hand.

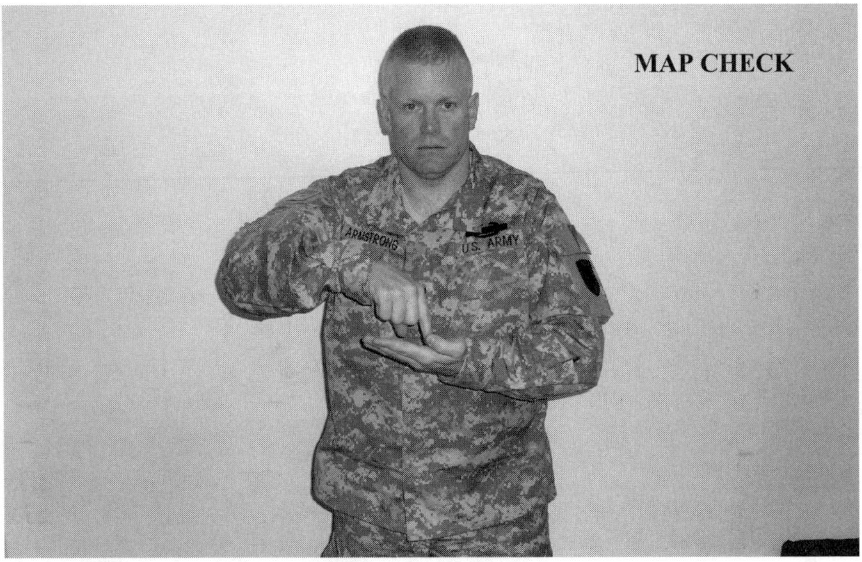

PACE COUNT: Tap the heel of boot repeatedly with an open hand.

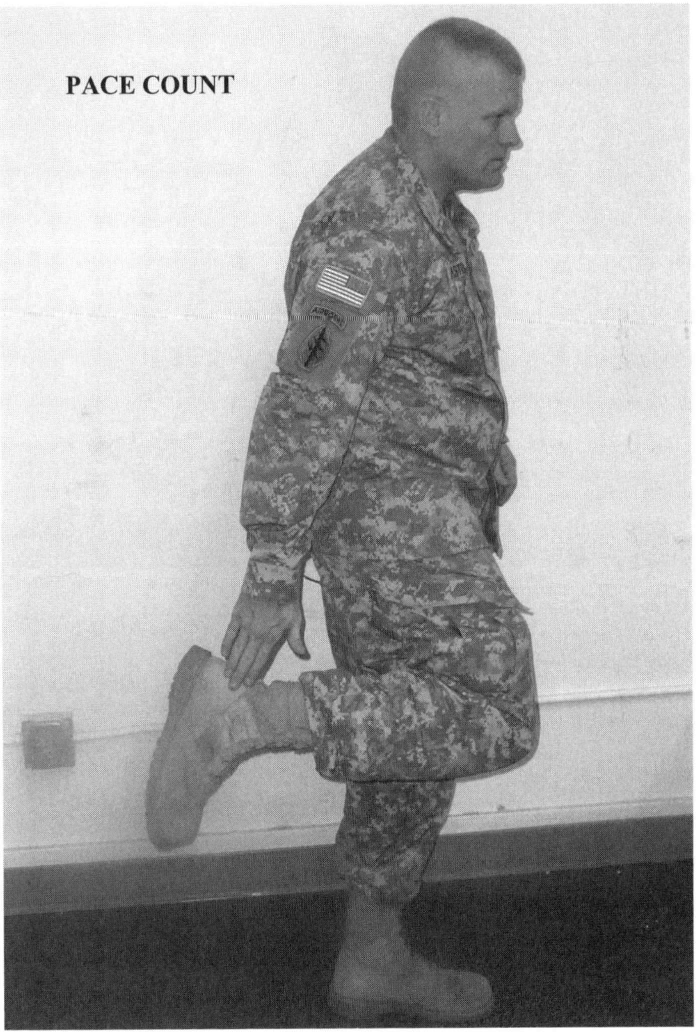

HEAD COUNT: Tap the back of the helmet repeatedly with an open hand.

HEAD COUNT

DANGER AREA: Draw the right hand, palm down, across the neck in a throat-cutting motion from left to right.

DANGER AREA

FREEZE: Raise the fist to head level.

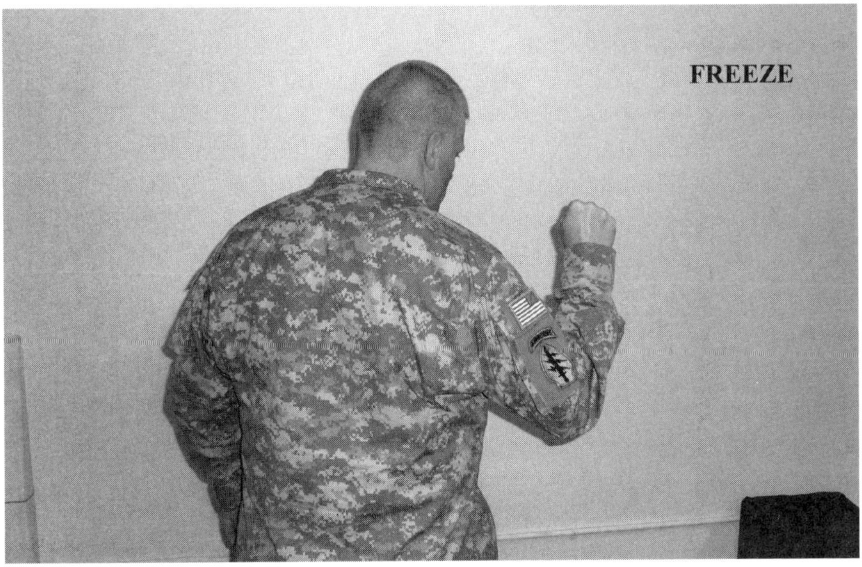

Other hand signals include, but are not limited, to the following:

ACTION (FRONT, RIGHT, LEFT, or REAR), FIGHT ON FOOT, or ASSAULT FIRE (DISMOUNTED TROOPS): Raise the fist to shoulder level and thrust it several times in the desired direction of action.

DISPERSE: Extend either arm vertically overhead; wave the arm and hand to the front, left, right, and rear with the palm toward the direction of each movement.

COIL: Raise one arm above the head and rotate it in a small circle.

BOUNDING OVERWATCH, COVER MY MOVE: Extend one arm to a 45-degree angle. Bend the arm and tap the helmet. Repeat.

NUCLEAR, BIOLOGICAL, CHEMICAL ATTACK: Extend the arms and fists. Bend the arms to the shoulders. Repeat.

RADIO-TELEPHONE OPERATOR FORWARD: Raise the hand to the ear with the thumb and little finger extended.

TRAVELING: Extend the arm overhead and swing it in a circle from the shoulder.

Chapter 12

Officer Branch Information

"Wheresoever you go, go with all your heart."

— Confucius

Branches of the Army are broken down into three categories: Combat Arms, Combat Support, and Combat Service Support. I have left out special branches like the Chaplin Corps, Jag Corps, and Medical Service Corps. Special branches do not require OCS because they are direct commission.

Combat Arms

Infantry

The Infantry forms the nucleus of the Army's fighting strength. Its mission: To maintain a state of readiness in preparation for combat worldwide. Often described as "the best lay psychiatrist in the world," the Infantry officer must savor the challenges that come from total involvement with his soldiers. He must know his men, their problems, their needs—and get them all working together.

Field Artillery

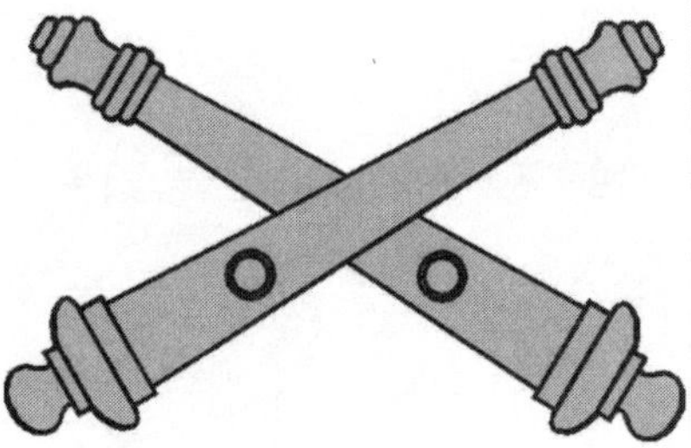

The Field Artillery is the Army's Fire Support branch—the "King of Battle." Its leaders must destroy, neutralize, or suppress the enemy by cannon, rocket, or missile fire and integrate all supporting fires—Field Artillery, tactical air, Naval guns, Army aviation, and mortars—into combined-arms operations. Field Artillerymen put "Steel on Target" in the right places, at the right time and in the right proportions to assure the success of the maneuver commander's plan—a task that requires thorough understanding of maneuver and fire support doctrine, tactics, and techniques.

Armor

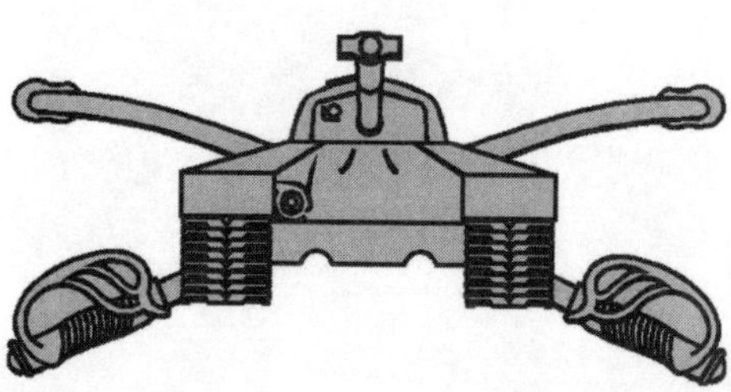

The heritage and spirit of the United States Horse Cavalry lives in today's armor. Although the horse has been replaced by 60 tons of steel driven by a 1,500 HP engine, the dash and daring of the cavalry still roams today's battlefields. This branch is one of the Army's most versatile combat arms. It is continually evolving to meet worldwide challenges and potential threats.

Special Forces

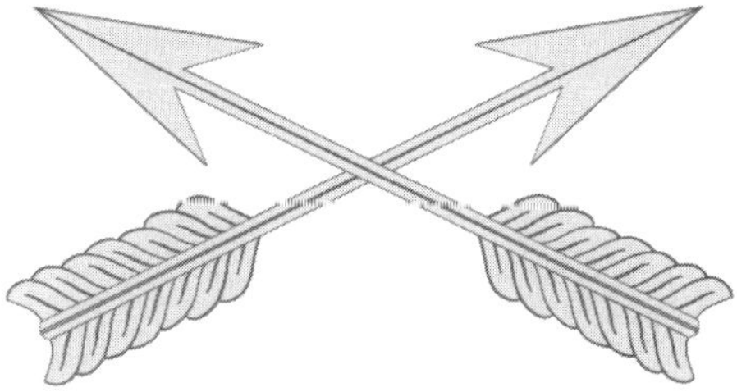

The mission of Special Forces (SF) is special reconnaissance, direct action, foreign internal defense, unconventional warfare, and counter-terrorism. Simply put, SF does things for the U.S. Army that typically do not make headlines. Their funding is separate from the rest of the Army and is typically much higher than normal line units. SF are selective of those who want to re-branch. If approved, SF candidates attend a three week Special Forces Assessment and Selections program (SFAS). If an officer completes SFAS and their branch career course, they attend the 26-week Special Forces Detachment Officer Qualification Course (SFDOQC or Q-course). Upon completion, SF Captains are branch qualified and ready to serve the Special Forces branch.

Don't worry about going SF right now. Complete OCS and your Officer Basic Course, get some troop time, and in a few years if you possess the motivation and the right mind frame, look up your nearest SF recruiter.

Combat Support

Chemical

Today's lethal battlefield demands officers who possess expertise in nuclear, biological, chemical, smoke, and flame operations. Chemical officers fill this vital role. Whether you are a chemical corps lieutenant in a combat arms battalion or a chemical corps colonel making critical recommendations to the corps commander, you will play an invaluable part in winning on tomorrow's battlefield.

Engineer

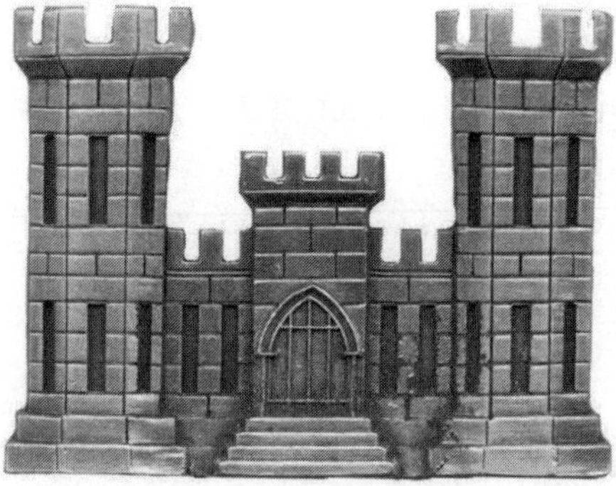

All engineer officers receive troop leading experience in combat, construction, or topographic engineering units before branching out into such fields as civil works, military construction, environmental engineering, and other specialties. Combat missions for engineers include: bridge building and destruction, minefield emplacement and reduction, route clearing, and other tasks requiring specialized engineer skills and equipment. Construction engineers build and maintain roads, airfields, and facilities to support combat operations. Topographic engineers provide the terrain depiction products and analyses that give maneuver commanders an edge in battle.

Civil Affairs

Civil Affair (CA) officers reside primarily within the Army Reserves. Their primary mission is liaison with foreign nationals, governments, and the military of countries in which the U.S. military and/or our allies caused a “displacement” through military action. CA personnel played a role in replacing the communist government in Grenada post-Operation Urgent Fury by helping build an operational government. Today, CA units are being deployed more than at anytime in their history. CA officers face real world challenges on a daily basis while in service to the U.S. Army during wartime and in peace.

Military Intelligence

Military Intelligence (MI) officers are primarily concerned with the intelligence aspects of the Army's overall mission. They specialize in intelligence, counterintelligence, cryptology, signal intelligence, electronic warfare, operational security, order of battle, interrogation, aerial surveillance, imagery interpretation, and all related planning. While on a staff, MI officers fill the S2 billet and act as the primary intelligence officer for the commander. MI officers contribute greatly to the Army mission at home and abroad.

Military Police

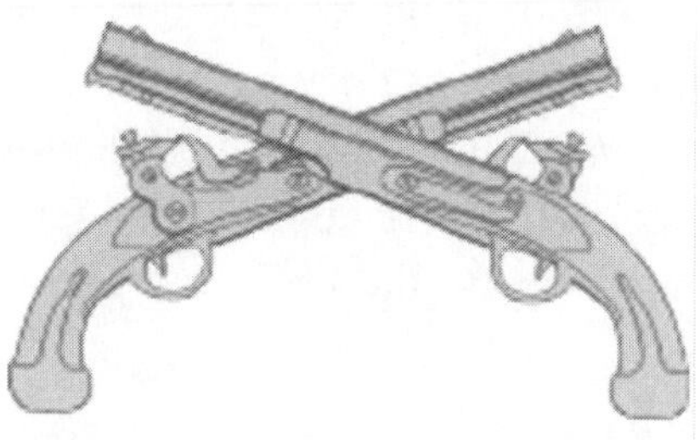

Military Police Corps (MP) members normally support battlefield operations by opposing enemy forces to the rear of the main effort. Collection and processing of enemy prisoners of war and evacuating them for the forward area are specific missions they fulfill for the Army. Once the battle is won, the MP Corps provides security over facilities and resources critical to the Army's mission.

Signal Corps

The overall mission of the Signal Corps includes the collective, integrated, and synchronized use of information technology in the form of systems, networks, services, and resources supporting command, control, communications, and computer requirements in organizations at all operational levels. Simply put, the Signal Corps keeps the Army commanders in contact with all of their key elements during peacetime, wartime, and during contingency operations other than war.

Combat Service Support

Adjutant General Corps

The AG Corps mission is to help build and sustain combat readiness through planning, operating, and managing all military personnel activities to include: readiness; strength reporting; casualty operations; replacement management; information management; postal operations; morale, welfare, and recreation support; and personnel services.

Finance Corps

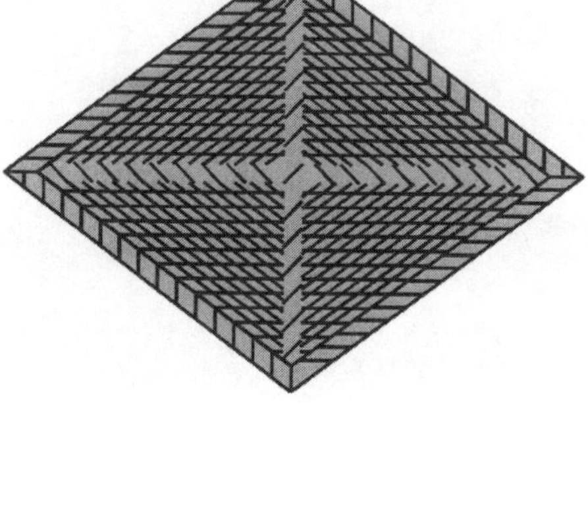

The ultimate mission of the Finance Corps is to sustain the combat soldier and commanders in the field with timely and accurate finance and accounting support. This support includes military and civilian pay, the preparation and payment of travel, transportation, and commercial vendor vouchers, and accounting for the obligation and disbursement of public funds.

Ordnance Corps

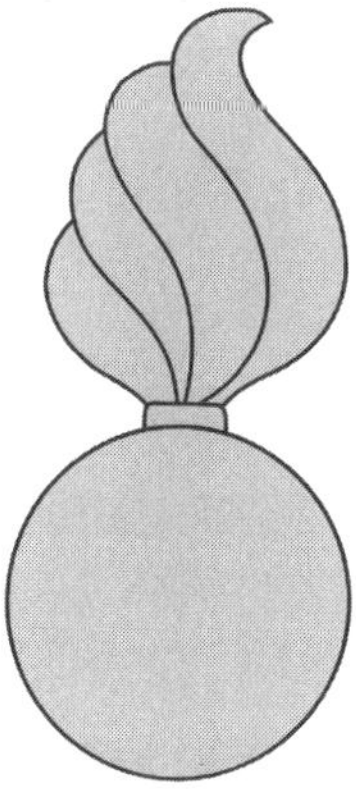

The purpose of the Ordnance Corps is to support the development, production, acquisition, and sustainment of weapons systems and munitions, and to provide Explosive Ordnance Disposal, during peace and war, to provide superior combat power to current and future forces of the United States Army.

Quartermaster Corps

Logistics Officers (QM) provide focused logistics support to sustain the Army in any and all theaters of operations at home or abroad. Today's Army needs professional officers at all stages of combat service and support. Computing requirements for missile repair parts or operating a petroleum pipeline to keep the combat arms and transportations corps fed are just a few examples of what the Quartermaster Corps may be asked to do.

Transportation Corps

The primary purpose of the TC is to provide transportation services to the Army, the Department of Defense, and other government agencies in peace and war. They also have a hand in the development of transportation concepts and doctrine while performing transportation unit operations, to include truck, boat, rail, and trailer/cargo transfer operations.

The TC also has a hand in all troop and equipment movements into and out of theaters of operation. In order for combat arms soldiers to take the fight to the enemy, they need their equipment and supplies on site. This is the main objective behind the Transportation Corps.

Summary

While each branch officer believes in his or her heart that their specific branch is the best in the Army, the reality is that the military could not function without all these various branches working together. Everyone has a job to do. Every branch has a specific task and purpose in support of each other and the overall operation of the U.S. Army.

Selection of a branch upon graduation will depend on a number of details. The first is the needs of the Army. Branch selection considerations will be different for active duty graduates versus reserve/national guard graduates because the need of the Army will be different on a Federal level when compared to state level. I highly recommend you speak with a branch selection specialist prior to attending OCS. The best case scenario is that you have your top three branches in mind prior to beginning OCS.

Chapter 13

What to Take, What to Leave Home

"Five seconds of keeping your mouth shut is worth an hour of explanation."

—Kevin Miller

There are many things you need to do and arrange before you leave for OCS. This chapter discusses many of these important issues, as well as what to take to OCS and what to leave home.

Financial and Personal Obligations

Before you leave for OCS, either square away your financial situation or have someone you trust take care of your financial and personal obligations. It is important that you set aside some quiet time to write down your financial obligations so that others who have access to your affairs who are helping you fully understand them.

It might be a good idea to grant someone you trust a Power of Attorney to handle your financial accounts. This will allow them to sign checks for you, pay bills, and so forth. However, giving someone a Power of Attorney carries with it important legal ramifications. If you are thinking about using this option, make sure and speak to an attorney first.

It is also important that you write down your non-financial (personal) obligations so that others who are handling your affairs understand the day-to-day things you would do if you were still home.

This could include everything from taking care of a house pet to checking in on an ailing friend or relative.

Be sure to have a back-up plan should your original plan fail. Also, if you are a reserve or national guard soldier, be sure to tell your employer when you will be leaving for OCS, how long you will be gone, and provide a phone number for a friend or relative in case information needs to be relayed.

Luggage

Limit your luggage to one suitcase or duffle bag. That's it. You can take civilian clothes, but only a bare minimum—two or three slacks/shirt outfits at the most.

What to Bring to Officer Candidate School

S-1 / ADMINISTRATIVE-ISSUED ITEMS

- 1 each identification card/military card
- 1 pair of tags, Personnel ID w/ chain
- 1 each Drivers License (Mil / Civ)
- 1 each FM 3-21.8 (7-8) Infantry Rifle Platoon & Squad
- 5 copies each of orders: PH 1 (PH II, PH III — if state accelerated)

ISSUED CLOTHING

- 2 each belt, trousers
- 2 pair boots, combat/desert
- 1 pair boots, wet weather (overshoes)
- 2 each cap, Army Combat Uniform (ACU) w/name tape
- 1 each trousers, ECWS (Gore-Tex™)
- 1 each coat, cold weather, ACU or jacket, Gore-Tex
- 1 each coat/wet weather
- 1 pair gloves, shell, black leather w/ inserts
- 6 each coat, ACU with Velcro Name Tapes & Flag

- 1 each jacket, IPFU (Improved Physical Fitness Uniform)
- 1 pair pants, IPFU
- 1 each shirt, long sleeve, IPFU
- 2 each shirt, short sleeve, IPFU
- 2 each shorts, black, IPFU
- 1 each cap, knit, black (watch cap) or grey fleece
- 10 pair socks, wool, boot (green or black)
- 6 pair trousers, ACU
- 1 each trousers, wet weather
- 10 each undershirt, sand

INDIVIDUAL EQUIPMENT

- 1 each bag, duffel
- 1 each bag, sleeping (mummy or MSS—Mounted Soldier System)
- 1 each bag, waterproof
- 1 each bag, laundry
- 1 each belt, individual equipment
- 2 each canteen, water, plastic (1 qt.)
- 1 each case, first aid with field dressing case not required w/ LBV (load bearing vest)
- 2 each case, small arms not required w/LBV
- 1 each compass, lensatic with case & lanyard

FUNCTIONAL & MILITARY ISSUE

- 2 each cover, canteen
- 2 each cup
- 1 each Entrenching Tool w/carrier
- 1 each flashlight (w/all lenses and batteries)
- 2 each frame, strap, shoulder (ALICE) 1 left & right
- 1 each helmet, PASGT (Kevlar or Army Combat helmet (without cover)
- 1 set knee/elbow pads
- 1 each poncho

- 1 each liner, poncho
- 1 each map case, green or camo
- 1 each mat, sleeping
- 1 each ruck, ALICE, with frame (recommend large)
- 1 pair suspenders, individual equipment or tactical load bearing vest

ISSUED ITEMS

- 1 each bee-sting allergy kit (by prescription)
- 5 each bag, zip-lock, plastic (12 x 12)
- 5 each bag, zip-lock, plastic (8 x 8)
- 5 each bag, zip-lock, plastic (6 x 6)
- 1 pair plug, ear w/case
- 3 each pen, black, ball-point
- 2 each pen, Sharpie, fine point, black
- 1 each ruler, 12" clear
- 1 each sewing kit
- 2 each book, memo 3.5" x 4.5"
- 1 each marker, permanent, black
- 1 each notebook, steno type
- 2 packs index cards, 3" x 5" (100 per pack)
- 1 set pens, alcohol, super fine, red, blue, black, green
- 1 each pen, cleaning (alcohol)
- 2 each pencil, mechanical
- 2 each coordinate scale and protractor
- 1 each camouflage compact or stick
- 1 each calamine lotion
- 1 each chigg-away
- 1 each foot powder
- 1 each insect repellant
- 1 each lipstick, anti-chap
- 1 each pre-sun 15, 4 oz
- 1 each whistle, plastic, black or dark green
- 1 each camelback (color per AR 670-1) or 2 qt. canteen w/cover
- 1 each athletic supporter (male) w/cup

- 3 each brassiere, athletic/sports type (female)
- 1 shoeshine kit, desert boot cleaning kit
- 1 pair shoes, running (conservative in color)
- 1 pair shoes, shower (conservative in color)

COMMON ITEMS

- 2 pair laces, combat boot (spares)
- 25 feet parachute/550 cord
- 5 pair mid-calf socks, white, running (no logos or stripes)
- 1 role black electrical tape
- 1 set sand table kit for Phase II & III
- 1 pair eye protection (PPE). Must meet 2.87 safety standard
- 2 each tabs, blousing (velcro)
- 1 kit toilet articles, (as required): toothbrush
- case, toothpaste, soap, soap dish, shaving gear, mirror, comb or small brush, feminine hygiene articles, dental floss, mouthwash, antiperspirant. No electric razors (check with regiment).
- 4 each towel, bath, white or brown
- 2 each washcloth, white or brown
- 10 each underwear, white, black, brown, or sand
- 3 each padlock, combination (serviceable, must fit on duffle bag)
- 1 each watch, wrist (black/green/sand)
- 1 pair blousing rubbers (elastic with hooks)
- 10 each coat hangers, copper
- 2 pair government-issued eyeglasses w/strap (if required by prescription; no contacts) 1 pair to wear and 1 extra
- 1 set civilian clothes (worn in transit)
- 4 each battery, D cell (2 in flashlight)
- Money. Do not bring a large amount to OCS. You will need to cover any prescriptions and a few incidentals. Reimbursement will be thru TRICARE/Line of Duty (LOD) procedures/policies.

OPTIONAL ITEMS

- 1 pair boots, ECWS (Gore-Tex™) or extra pair of boots

- 3 each long sleeve T-shirt, sand
- Cold weather under armor top and bottoms may replace polypro
- 2 each top, underwear, polypropylene
- 2 each bottom, underwear, polypropylene

What NOT to Bring to Officer Candidate School

- Tobacco products (including smokeless tobacco)
- Alcohol
- Any supplements taken to enhance performance
- Medications not prescribed by a physician
- Contact lenses
- Cosmetics
- Hair nets and curlers
- Perfumes, colognes, or after-shave
- Body sprays, aerosol products, lighters
- Electric or battery operated razors
- Digital/tape recorders, CD players, Walkman, MP3 players
- Radios, portable TV/ DVD players
- Cellular phones*
- Pagers, beepers
- Laptop/palmtop computers
- Global positioning devices
- Magazines
- Newspapers
- Bayonets, fixed-blade knives, or knives with a blade over 3"
- Perfumed or scented lotions (unscented lotions are not prohibited)
- Any handheld electronic devices (i.e., video game players, palm pilot, organizers)
- Adult material of any kind
- Vitamins
- Personal Firearms

* Cell phones may be authorized at a later date as a privilege for performance. You may bring your cell phone to OCS, but it will probably be stored at first with

your personal gear in a locked room. To be sure, check with Ft. Benning OCS or your State RTI prior to shipping to OCS.

Chapter 14

Top Seven Mistakes You Will NOT Make

"Quitters never win. Winners never quit."

— Virginia Hutchinson

You will make many mistakes during OCS. Expect that it will happen and it won't be such a shock and disappointment when it happens. The only question is who will learn quickly from his or her mistakes, and who will need "extra training." Below is a list I created of the seven most common mistakes candidates make during OCS. Read it carefully so you can avoid all or most of them.

1. *Spotlight Ranger*

This is the candidate who shines while in leadership and in front of the TAC staff, but when the real work needs to be done he/she is nowhere to be found (or is simply lazy). Typically, candidates will police this person up through peer pressure or hit them hard during the three peer evaluations. If the TAC staff gets the impression you are a "Spotlight Ranger," be prepared to suffer more stress and responsiblities. Remember: YOU are not a "Spotlight Ranger."

2. *Honor Code Violation*

Cheating or failing to report someone who is cheating will get you booted out of OCS. YOU will always be honest and you will NOT tolerate anyone who is not.

3. *Failure to Prepare Self and Equipment*

There is more to being fit for OCS than running, pushing, and crunches. There are 5-, 7-, and 10-mile road marches that can destroy the feet of the under-prepared. YOU will always be prepared because you have read this book. You will make sure your boots are broken in before the long marches, and you will be in good shape and take care of yourself. (See Chapter 6)

4. *Family Care Plan*

This covers everything from a sick child to a Dear John letter. You will have very little time to focus on anything but your training. YOU will take care of personal/home matters before you ship out to OCS.

5. *Failure to Cope with Atmosphere*

Many former NCOs who have had very successful military careers up to time they begin OCS will be treated as harshly as everyone else. Once a soldier is accepted to OCS and pins on the OCS rank, he or she is "in training" to become a second lieutenant. Expect the rough treatment and embrace what the TAC staff is trying to teach you. YOU know that everything is done for a reason. You will never quit. Quitting when the going gets tough is not a trait the military is looking for in its leaders. If you quit at something and then try again, the TAC staff will never forget it. You will have a more difficult time on the second attempt because the staff is going to make sure you have the will and the character to finish. YOU will never quit at anything you are asked to do.

6. *Sick Call Ranger*

Candidates who spend each morning at sick call for aches and pains rather than at PT with their classmates are what we call "Sick Call Rangers." Federal OCS and Fast Track OCS have sick call every morning during scheduled PT. I have seen soldiers get brought up on malingering charges for spending too much time at sick call. If you are truly too unhealthy to attend OCS without going to sick call every day, do not attempt OCS. You will bring the rest of your classmates down. If you are using sick call as a way to get out of PT, you suffer from a lack of integrity and you have no place in the Army, much less the officer corps. YOU will not be a "Sick Call Ranger."

7. *Backdoor DOR*

At each "gate" (the transitions between basic to intermediate to senior phase) you will be tempted to quit, take some time off, and start again when the next session catches up because you have completed a phase and do not have to repeat it for up to one year. I have seen this too many times in State OCS. Candidate "John Smith" attends State Fast Track with the intent of finishing the 9-week course and returning to his state to pin on gold bars. That plan falls apart when OC John Smith reaches the end of Phase I and misses home. He has second thoughts about State Traditional OCS (one weekend per month until Phase III). "I could be home in two days, sleeping in my own bed," thinks OC Smith.

YOU will not make this mistake. Why? Because you have read this book and know that the gates are in place for injured candidates or those who have real emergencies—not candidates who miss home. YOU will not use a transition period to quit. If you quit when the going gets tough, what are you going to do in combat? Wars are not fought one-weekend per month and during two weeks in the summer. YOU will suck it up and finish strong. And you will always be thankful that you did.

Chapter 15

Role of TAC NCO

"You will never be a leader unless you first learn to follow and be led."

— Tiorio

Charge of the Noncommissioned Officer

I will discharge carefully and diligently the duties of the grade to which I have been promoted and uphold the traditions and standards of the Army. I understand that soldiers of lesser rank are required to obey my lawful orders. Accordingly, I accept responsibility for their actions. As a noncommissioned officer, I accept the charge to observe and follow the orders and directions given by supervisors acting according to the laws, articles, and rules governing the discipline of the Army, I will correct conditions detrimental to the readiness thereof. In so doing, I will fulfill my greatest obligation as a leader and thereby confirm my status as a noncommissioned officer.

The "Charge of the Noncommissioned Officer" applies today as much as the day it was written. The role of the Noncommissioned Officer (NCO) in the Army has not changed much over the years. Training is NCO business and the role the TAC NCO executes during OCS fits exactly with their charge. NCOs are subject matter experts on soldiering skills. They are tasked at OCS to keep TAC officers from making fools of themselves in front of candidates while always showing candidates what "right" looks like. Hopefully, TAC NCOs will impress upon the future Second Lieutenants under their guidance what their future platoon sergeant should be doing once they get to their units.

In years past, a TAC NCO handed out spot corrections and smoke sessions just like the TAC officers. Their role was to mentor candidates while also mentoring TAC officers. This was a familiar role for the NCO corps. Recently, the TAC NCO began to play more the role of mentor and less the role of spot corrector. Spot corrections are still made with candidates, but the NCO does it with less yelling and fewer smoke sessions. At some RTIs, the TAC NCO at the platoon level acts as a First Sergeant and spends a large amount of time coordinating training events and ensuring the candidates have made the right synchronization.

Personally, I do not agree with the latest role the TAC NCO fills. There are always times in an officer's career when he or she will be on the receiving end of a senior NCO's vehement disagreement, especially as a junior officer. If he or she gets the idea that the main role of the NCO corps is to "make sure chow is served and bullets are available," they are missing 98% of what the NCO corps is all about.

If a TAC NCO chooses not to "get in the ass" of a candidate, then I have absolutely zero issue with that. As TACs, we all have our personal way of handling situations. However, I do not like the idea of instructing NCOs not to be vociferous in all they do. This goes against the role of the NCO.

Chapter 16

Company Leadership Positions

"Leadership is action, not position."

— Donald H. McGannon

Officer candidates occupy all of the command and leadership positions within the OCS Company. A normal rating period is 24 to 48 hours in length. However, rating periods during Phase II, Phase III, or Senior Phase are situational dependant and can be at the discretion of the TAC Staff.

Company Commander (CO)

1. General Duties: The Candidate Company Commander is responsible for everything the Company does or fails to do. He/she plans, makes timely decisions, issues orders, delegates tasks, and personally supervises company activities. The primary responsibility of the student commander is to gain and maintain control of the company and set the example for his/her company.

2. The Candidate Commander exercises command through the Candidate Executive Officer (XO), Candidate First Sergeant (1SG), and Candidate Platoon Leaders (PL's).

3. The Candidate Commander is responsible for the morale, welfare, control, and discipline of the company. He/she will:

- Supervise the XO and 1SG in accomplishing their missions.
- Supervise PL's in supporting and enforcing all standards, policies, and procedures set forth in the OCS program. Take positive action to correct deficiencies.
- Be responsible for all status reports.
- Move the Company to and from instruction areas in a military manner.
- Enforce all policies and procedures for proper conduct of course.
- The CO must know his duties, responsibilities, and actions IAW FM 3- 21.5 (Drill & Ceremony).
- When training at platoon level the CO will attend all training periods with his platoon.
- In the absence of specific instructions, guidance, or orders, the CO will make those decisions necessary to accomplish the mission in accordance with established procedures, safety considerations, and common sense.

4. The CO maintains the CO's book and has it ready for inspection at all times. The CO's book will be neat, presentable, and updated. At a minimum, it will include the following:

- Medical Evacuation Procedures
- Emergency First-Aid Procedures
- Training Schedule
- DFAC Menu and Schedule
- Daily Weather Information, with Wet Bulb Information, if applicable
- Current OC Roster
- TAC Duty Roster to include building numbers, room numbers, and phone numbers
- Installation Maps (Cantonment and Tactical)
- Relevant Installation telephone and building numbers
- Tabbed FM 3-21.5 (Drill and Ceremony)
- Tabbed FM 21-20 (Physical Fitness Training)

- AR 670-1 (Wear and Appearance of Army Uniforms and Insignia)
- AR 25-50 (Preparing and Managing Correspondence)
- Will be regiment-dependent

Executive Officer (XO)

1. General Duties: The XO is the principal assistant to the Candidate Commander. The XO should do everything possible to relieve the Commander of administrative burdens through the proper management of his resources.

2. The XO acts as the chief advisor to the Commander and assumes command to the Company in the absence of the commander.

3. The XO coordinates with the principal instructor for each block of instruction before scheduled training for any special requirements. Upon receiving those instructions, he will report to the CO.

4. The XO coordinates with the TAC Company Commander and food service manager for special and ordinary mess needs, including special rations, changes in mess times, and amendments to and implementation of dining facility policies.

5. The XO coordinates with the TAC Company Commander and TAC Company Executive Officer for arms issue and turn-in. The XO supervises all supply operations and arrangements.

6. The XO monitors heat categories and other natural dangers, which threaten warm-weather training, and reports any dangers up the chain-of-command immediately.

7. The XO must know his duties, responsibilities, and actions in accordance with FM 3-21.5 (D&C).

8. The XO is responsible for barracks and building security to include the location of all keys.

9. The XO is responsible for all sensitive items.

10. The XO will ensure that all Officer Candidates report for formal counseling (Performance Counseling) with a Self-Assessment Report (SAR).

11. The XO maintains the XO's book and has it ready for inspection at all times. The XO's book will be neat, presentable, and updated. At a minimum, it includes the following:

- Medical Evacuation Procedures
- Emergency First-Aid Procedures
- Training Schedule
- DFAC Menu and Schedule
- Daily Weather Information, with Wet Bulb Information, if applicable
- Current OC Roster
- TAC Duty Roster to include building numbers, room numbers, and phone numbers
- Installation Maps (Cantonment and Tactical)
- Relevant Installation telephone and building numbers
- Tabbed FM 3-21.5 (Drill and Ceremony)
- Tabbed FM 21-20 (Physical Fitness Training)
- AR 670-1 (Wear and Appearance of Army Uniforms and Insignia)
- AR 25-50 (Preparing and Managing Correspondence)
- Dependent on regiment

First Sergeant (1SG)

1. General Duties: The 1SG monitors and coordinates control of all matters pertaining to logistical requirements and administrative

actions. Active communication and supervision through the Platoon Sergeants is essential; however, this communication will complement the formal chain-of-command not circumvent it.

2. Accountability: Accountability of all soldiers is an essential and constant process of updates. The 1SG will maintain an accurate accountability status report at all times. (This will be defaulted to the PSG when platoon level training is incurred.) The 1SG will prepare a report of the Company accountability and submit it to the Company TAC or his representative.

This report will be updated following formations or changes in personnel status. This report should be generated prior to formation whenever possible to provide for time constraints. PSGs will make an informal report to include any OCs not present for duty and the reason for their absence. The completed report will include:

- Number of OCs Assigned
- Number of OCs Present
- Names of absent OCs
- Reason OC is absent
- Estimated time of return for absent OCs

3. The 1SG will form the company and receive report IAW FM 3-21.5, Chapter 7.

4. The 1SG must set the example for all NCOs.

5. The 1SG must know his duties, responsibilities, and actions IAW FM 3-21.5 (D&C).

6. The 1SG must monitor and coordinate all mess, logistics, and company administration needs with the XO.

7. When training is conducted at platoon level, the 1SG will train with his platoon.

8. The 1SG will ensure at least one police call is conducted of his company area during his tour of duty.

Platoon Leader (PL)

1. General Duties: The PL commands the platoon and is responsible for the morale, welfare, and discipline of his subordinates. The platoon leader is ultimately responsible for everything the platoon does or fails to do.

2. The PL commands primarily through Squad Leaders (SL), delegating authority through the Platoon Sergeant.

3. The PL must set the example for his platoon.

4. The PL must know his duties, responsibilities, and actions IAW FM 3-21.5 (D&C).

5. The platoon leader will ensure that:

- Proper accountability is maintained.
- PSG and SLs fulfill their responsibilities.
- Platoon members receive necessary information for the platoon to accomplish assigned missions.
- An equitable distribution of details and privileges exists and OC's personal needs are taken care of.
- SLs inspect their squads before each formation and correct deficiencies.
- OCs are spot-checked for appearance, required knowledge, and preparedness for training.
- Platoon TAC Officers receive daily briefings of the status of the platoon. This briefing includes, but is not limited to, morale, personnel problems, inspection results, anticipated problems, and planned courses of action for improving platoon performance.

- OCs inspect weapons, maintain accountability of all sensitive items, and platoon equipment before and during training, and before turn-in.
- A Platoon notebook is maintained with an annotated platoon roster, broken down by squad.
- Spot checks soldiers prior to movement.

Platoon Sergeant (PSG)

1. General Duties: The PSG is the principle assistant to the platoon leader and will assume command of the platoon in the absence of the platoon leader.

2. The PSG must know his duties, responsibilities, and actions IAW FM 3-21.5 (D&C).

3. The PSG monitors and coordinates all logistical and administrative needs with the 1SG.

4. The PSG will:

- Maintain accurate accountability of platoon members.
- Maintain sensitive items and platoon equipment at all times and keep the chain-of-command informed of the accountability status.
- Conduct formations in accordance with FM 3-21.5 and the OC Guide.
- Enforce the regulations and directives of OCS.
- Ensure the platoon maintains and accounts for assigned equipment at all times.
- Relay pertinent information to the platoon in a timely manner.
- Maintain control of and ensure compliance of all SOPs.
- Assist the PL in conducting inspections.
- Ensure the platoon bulletin board is up to date.
- Spot check soldiers prior to movement.

Squad Leader (SL)

1. General Duties: The SL is the direct supervisor of the individual squad members.

2. The SL must know his duties, responsibilities, and actions IAW FM 3-21.5 (D&C).

3. The SL will ensure that:

- Squad status is maintained, including the location and activity of members.
- Squad members maintain and account for all issued property.
- Personal appearance, uniform appearance, and personal hygiene of all squad members are to the highest possible standards.
- The squad is prepared to accomplish assigned missions.
- The squad's billeting area is inspection-ready at all times.
- The squad completes all details to the highest standards possible.
- Each OC knows the mission to be accomplished and the required knowledge material.
- All squad members are informed.
- Conduct pre-combat checks and pre-combat inspections (PCC/PCI).

Chapter 17

How to . . .

"Example is leadership."

— Dr. Albert Schweitzer

This chapter offers a number of important things you need to know and understand BEFORE you arrive at Officer Candidate School. Read this chapter, and then read it again.

Who to Salute

Salute all Warrant and Commissioned officers while out of doors (except while in the field) upon recognition. When you are inside, you salute only while reporting or during ceremonies. If you are in front of a formation, call the formation to "attention" and then turn in the direction of the ranking officer and give the greeting of the day. At times, this will take place on a parade field and the ranking officer is 150 meters away. Do it anyway. While OCS is the only place you will practice this irregular exercise, it helps build attention to detail in you and with the other candidates. Attention to detail comes in very handy throughout OCS and during your Army career.

Proper greetings are determined by local time:

- Morning is from 0001 to 1159.
- Afternoon is from 1200 to 1659.
- Evening is from 1700 to 2400.

- All greetings are concluded with sir or ma'am, as appropriate.

How to Wear OCS Rank

Patrol cap and Helmet: OCS insignia is centered left to right and top to bottom on the front of the patrol cap.

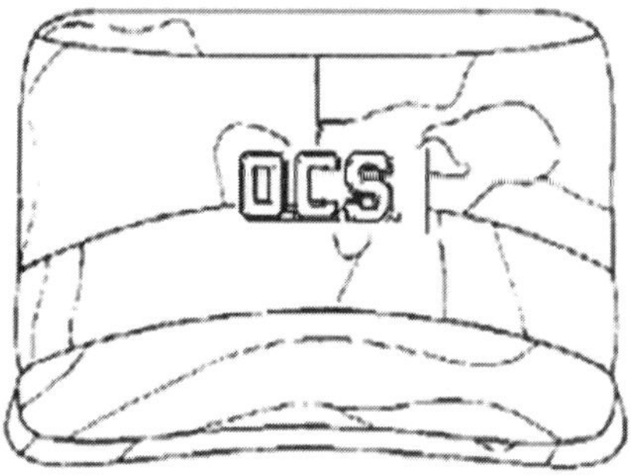

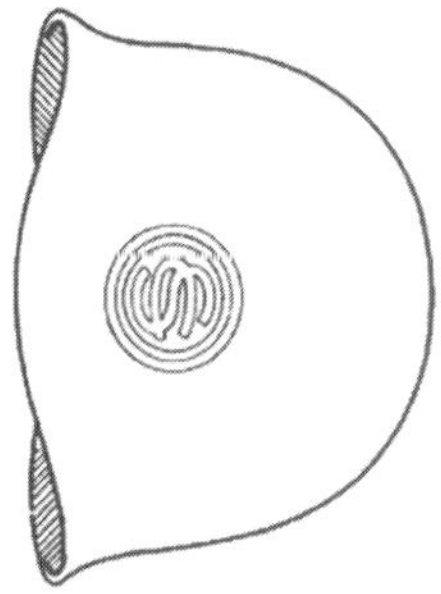

ACU: Sterile minus American flag on right shoulder and OCS rank on chest. (Could vary depending on OCS regiment and commander's discretion.)

Class A Uniform: Class A uniform is worn the same as prior to attending OCS. During basic and intermediate phase, the uniform will be sterile. When you reach the senior phase, ascots will be added as well as any service awards or badges. (These could vary depending on OCS regiment and commander's discretion.)

How to Make Your Bed

A hospital corner is a corner of a made-up bed in which the sheets have been neatly and securely folded. During OCS you will be required to have a neatly made bed at all times. Any beds that do not conform to the OCS standard will likely get tossed during routine inspections by TAC staff. And then, you only have to make it again. Make it right the first time and every time.

How to make your bed, step by step:

1. Pick up the edge of the sheet about 15 inches from the foot of the bed.

2. Lift up the sheet so it makes a diagonal fold.

3. Lay the fold on the mattress.

4. Take the part of the sheet that is hanging and tuck it underneath the mattress.

5. Drop the fold, pull it smooth, and tuck that under the mattress as well.

6. Turn the top of the sheet over the top of the blanket near where your head rests.

7. Place pillows under blanket and pull sheet tight.

Pass In-Ranks Inspection

Ensure the CO, 1SG, XO, PL, and PSG all meet the inspection standard. Assign teams to review what "right" looks like uniform by uniform. Ensure that every soldier meets the same standard.

Example: Platoon in-ranks inspection

The Battalion commander will more than likely check the progress of the current OCS class, and what better way is there to do this than with an in-ranks inspection. The PL will know the inspection is coming either by reading ahead in the schedule or being told by the TAC staff. (This is a critical event on the Blue card.) Below are some tips for passing inspection:

- Rehearse with the platoon the commands, "open ranks, march," and "dress right, dress."
- Keep the uniform as simple as possible; do not add items unnecessarily.
- Utilize chain of command (CO down to team leaders) to ensure uniformity.
- Rehearse, rehearse, and rehearse some more.

Pass Barracks Inspection

Ensure the CO, 1SG, XO, PL, and PSG all meet the inspection standard. Assign teams to inspected areas in the bunk area. Example: latrines (male and female), common area, lockers, bunks, halls, and so on.

Example: Platoon Barracks Inspection

TAC staff can and will inspect the barracks at any given moment, so the barracks always need to be inspection-ready. However, there are also specific times when a barracks inspection will take place because it is planned in advance. Most of the time the TAC staff will offer something for passing the inspection, like moving to intermediate or senior phase, but this is not always the case. Below are some tips for passing inspection:

- Check the obvious areas first (latrine, windows for dust, the tops of lockers).
- Assign teams to set up bunk areas (see above).
- Use two sets of gear, one to use and one to display. Typically, TAC staff will allow one personal drawer or an extra room for securing extra gear.
- Do the floors and footwear display last. Make sure display items are clean.

* Regimental Officer Candidate Guide will dictate uniform display. In the mean time, this is what a locker and drawer display could look like.

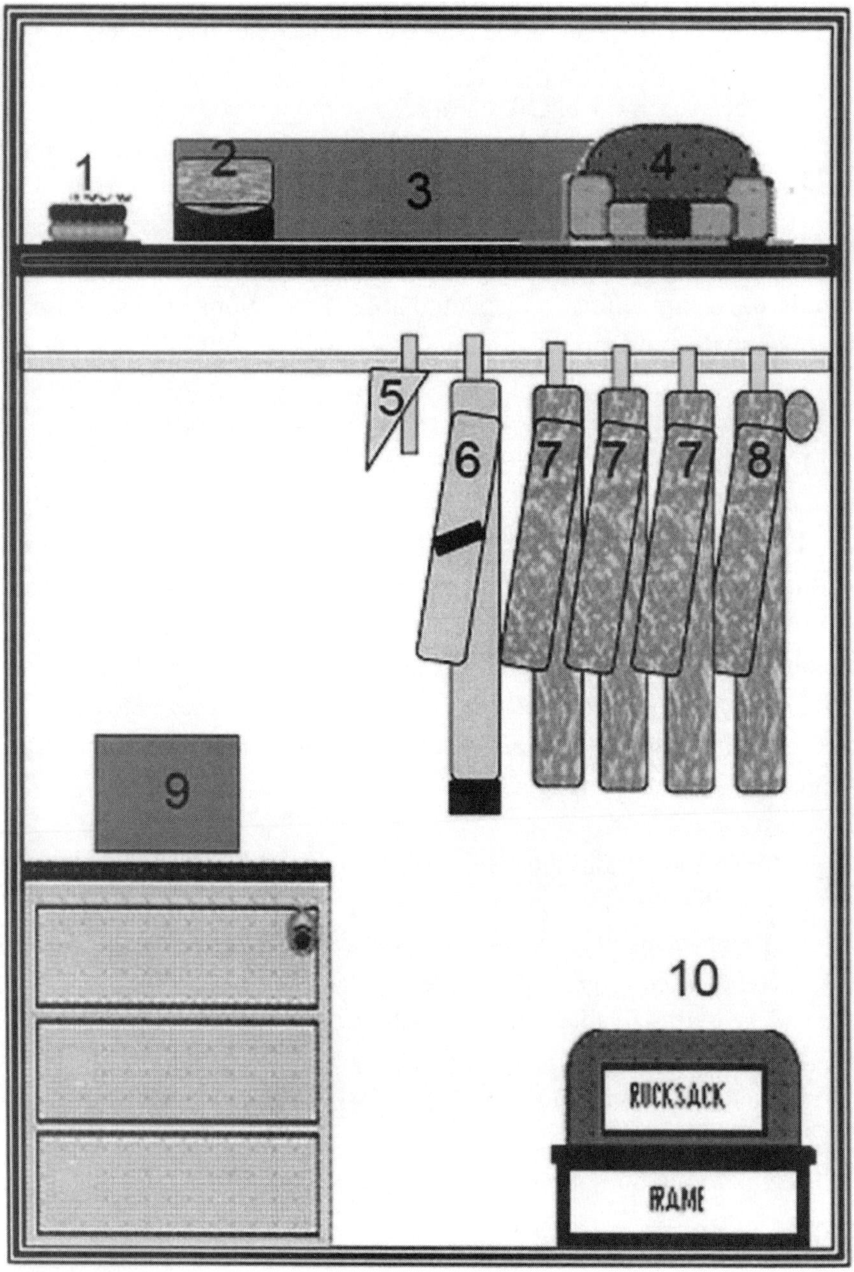

Wall Locker (from previous page)

1. Black leather gloves w/liners
2. ACU Patrol Cap w/Watch Cap
3. Sleep Pad
4. Helmet w/LBE
5. Ascot
6. IPFU Jacket and Pants
7. ACUs
8. Coat
9. Map Case
10. Rucksack

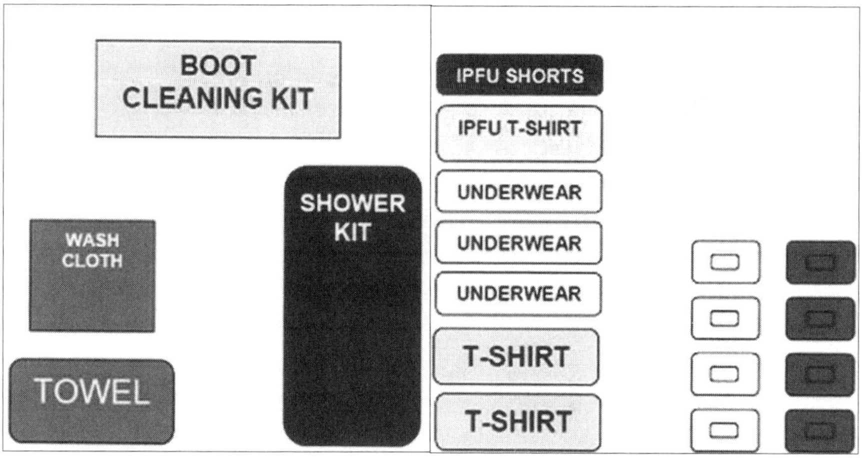

Equipment Inspection: "Junk on the Bunk"

Ensure that all gear is clean and displayed the same way. If there are candidates who do not have all the appropriate gear for display, do one of two things:

1. Ask permission to get them removed from the inspectable items list, or

2. Have one candidate write all of the missing item cards so they are as close to identical as possible.

See example on next page:

Class 54 OCS WAANG

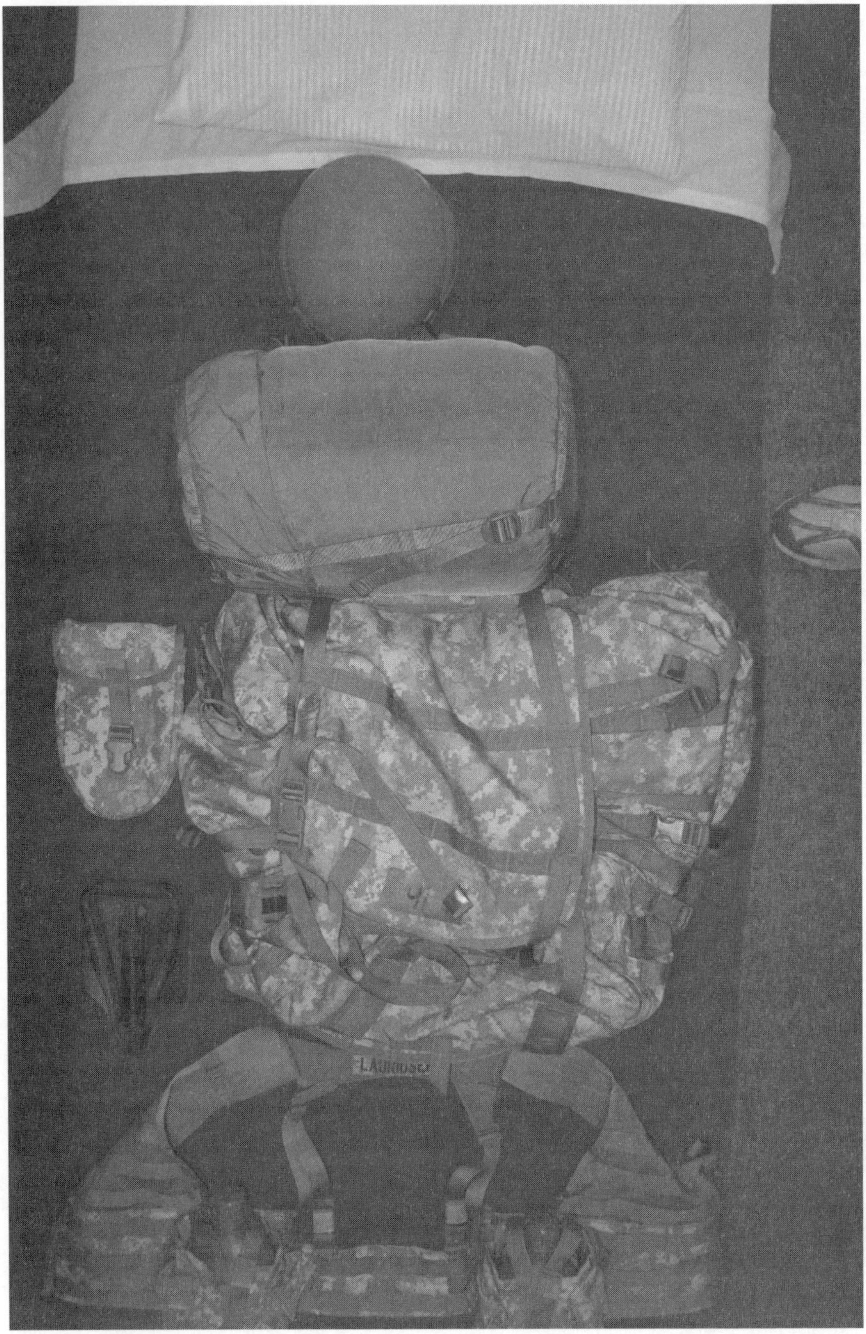

How to Prepare Class A and Blues Uniform for Commissioning

Reference AR-670-1

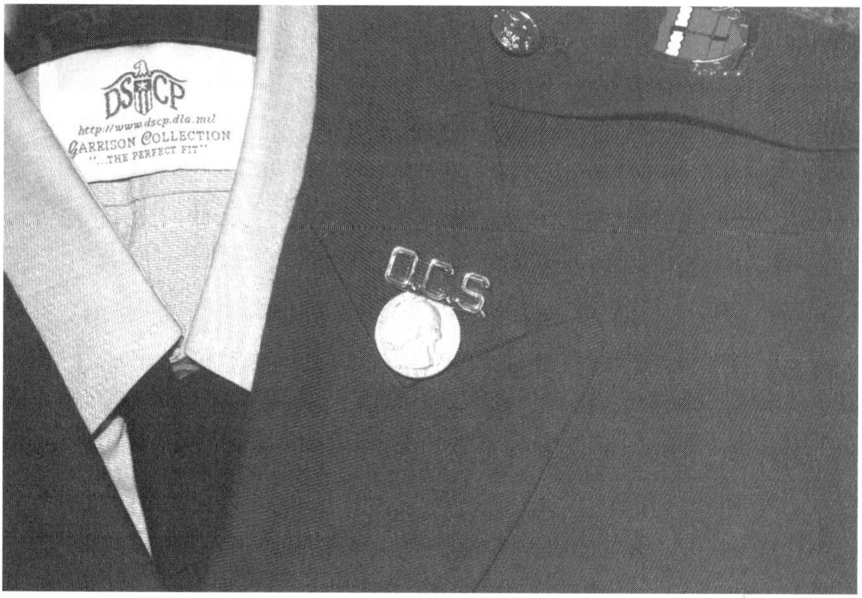

Class 54 OCS WAANG

The Class A and Dress Blues look equally sharp. The Army is still in the middle of transitioning from the Green Class A to a new Dress Blue. In the meantime, find out what the most current standard is for your commissioning source and prepare that uniform.

I prefer the skirt over the dress pants when it comes to female uniform. However, both look equally professional. Some commissioning sources will dictate one over the other. It is up to you to find out.

If you are prior enlisted and were issued green Class A uniforms at boot camp, you will need to purchase at least a new jacket. The material they use for basic issue is cheap. Invest in a new jacket and do your best to stay in it for the rest of your career. If you still fit in your basic issue pants, congratulations! However, you should still look into getting a new pair so your new jacket and pants are the same material. It will run more than $300 for the new uniform, but it is a small investment in the overall scheme of things.

How to Conduct an After-Action Review

The After-Action Review (AAR) is a structured review process that allows training participants to discover for themselves what happened, why it happened, and how it can be done better.

- Focus on the training objectives: Was the mission accomplished?
- Emphasize meeting Army standards (not who won or lost).
- Encourage soldiers to discover important lessons from the training event.
- Allow a large number of soldiers and leaders (including opposing force (OPFOR), aka, "the enemy") to participate so those lessons learned can be shared.

The AAR has four parts:

1. Review what was supposed to happen (training plan).

2. Establish what happened (to include OPFOR point of view).

3. Determine what was right or wrong with what happened.

4. Determine how the task should be done differently next time.

AAR Format:

1. Lane guide orientation

2. Friendly: Restate mission statement and concept of the operation (Squad Leader).

3. Enemy: Mission statement and concept of the operation (OPFOR).

4. Planning and Preparation Phase: Troop Leading Procedures.

5. Execution Phase: Line of Departure thru Change of Mission.

6. Ask squad members for comments.

7. Lane Guide/TAC comments/summary.

8. Conduct separate squad/platoon leader counseling.

9. Initiate movement to next lane SP or patrol base.

Chapter 18

Basic Training vs. Officer Candidate School

"The man who commands efficiently must have obeyed in the past."

— Cicero

Taking Orders

In basic training, Drill Sergeants give the orders, teach soldiers how to execute them, and soldiers learn and obey. Drill Sergeants ensure all movement times are met, accountability is always maintained, and training occurs to standard. At some basic training installations, Drill Sergeants will use "foul" language while working with the troops.

Giving Orders

At OCS, TACs staff provides training schedules and expectations, and the execution is the responsibility of the candidates. Everything candidates do or fail to do reflects on candidate leadership from the CO down through the lowest ranking squad leader. TAC staff will add stress and focus on teachable moments when necessary, but the program is designed so that the candidate leadership is responsible for the daily operations.

	APFT Minimum	Company leadership position	Basic Rifle Marksmanship (BRM)	Individual Task	Collective Tasks	Yelling	Peer Evaluation	TLPs	OPORD Creation	Field Leadership Exercise
OCS	180	X			X	X	X	X	X	X
Boot Camp	150		X	X		X				X

APFT: The minimum cumulative score to graduate Army boot camp and move to Advanced Individual Training (AIT) is 150. OCS requires a cumulative of 180. However, I highly recommend that, as a potential Officer Candidate, you consistently score above 230 to 250 because the stress and physical activity you endure will reduce your average. To calculate the raw pushup, sit-up, and two-mile run scores for your age bracket, reference the FM 21-20 (now the TC-3.22.20).

Company Leadership: Typically Drill Sergeants will assign platoon leadership while they act in the roles of Commander and First Sergeant. A Platoon Guide (PG) will be assigned and act as the pseudo Platoon Leader / Platoon Sergeant. They are rotated at the Drill Sergeant's discretion and are not rated. OCS has Commander down through Squad Leader assigned and all will be rated.

BRM: Boot Camp spends about two weeks on BRM. The closest a candidate gets to a live fire range at OCS is walking around the training area with blank ammo and blank fire adaptor on their individual weapon systems. No marksmanship is required with blank ammo.

Individual Tasks: Soldiers going through boot camp are tested on an individual basis. The measure is the "average soldier." Common tasks like treating a wound are gates for moving on in training. At OCS, there is training like first aid but they are not "GO, NO-GO" standards that will keep a candidate from moving on to the next phase. OCS is more about leadership and getting the group to succeed together.

Collective Tasks: Not so much at boot camp, at least not rated tasks. In OCS, almost all of the rated tasks (minus the Army Physical Fitness Test) are collective based tasks.

Yelling: Be prepared for some highly motivating screaming. Drill Sergeants and TACs are some of the best motivational speakers on this Earth.

Peer Evaluations: Evaluations at boot camp are purely Drill Sergeant driven. At OCS, candidates have three opportunities to evaluate their peers. These evaluations typically do not sink candidates. However, they can open the eyes of the TAC to issues occurring behind closed doors that could affect their next leadership rotation.

Troop Leading Procedures: While everything in the Army is steeped in the 8-TLP's, boot camp graduates are not tested on this specific topic, other than maybe memorization. At OCS, candidates are required to know and understand how the 8 TLP's integrate into the Army planning process.

OPORDs: Boot camp soldiers may have to memorize the format, but that is the extent. At OCS, everything is based on the five-paragraph order format. (Maybe WARNO or FRAGO).

Field Training Exercise (FTX): Both have a culminating FTX, with the only difference being soldier leadership at boot camp is not being rated individually, but it is at OCS.

Chapter 19

Composite Risk Management (CRM)

"Be sure you are right, then go ahead."

—Davy Crockett

As a leader, you will carry out the orders of those appointed above you. The orders will not always consider the safety of your troops as the top priority. It is up to you, the new lieutenant, to impress upon your soldiers the risks involved in any mission and how as a unit you will minimize, if not eliminate, those risks.

The following section provides you with the basic fundamentals of identifying risk, rating it, and mitigating as much of it as possible. Keep in mind that there is no one right answer. Each situation will dictate how risk can be averted.

Risk Mitigation during Training: There are four key principles in risk management while in a training environment or while in a combat zone:

> 1. *Integrate risk management into all training and combat missions from concept through termination.*
>
> Risk management principles need to be incorporated in the planning stage of any operation. An example of this would be to identify risks during a 7-mile road march. Consider the route, weather, packing list, time of day, and so forth. Is there risk associated with any of these four items? Start with the weather.

How can the weather create a potential hazard during the road march? Consider the heat. If it is warmer then 80 degrees, for example, the hot weather could pose the immediate hazards of dehydration and/or heat exhaustion for the soldiers participating on the road march.

2. *Accept zero needless risk.*

Now that you have identified the hazard, what can you do to minimize it? Elimination of the road march from the training schedule is not impossible. It needs to get done. It is up to the leadership to come up with ideas for minimizing hazards. Using the 7-mile march as an example, will forced hydration lower the risk? Yes. Forcing hydration prior to and during the road march will reduce the risk of dehydration and heat exhaustion. If possible, you could also minimize the risk by performing the road march during a cooler time of the day (like the early morning).

3. *Make risk decisions at the appropriate level.*

Once risk minimizing ideas are in place, permission will need to be granted for schedule changes above your pay grade. For example, moving the time of the company 7- mile road march will need to be approved by at least the company commander. However, an idea for minimizing the risk of dehydration (like forced hydration) prior to and during the road march can be approved and enforced at the platoon level.

4. *Document risk decisions.*

The risk assessment card is a documentation tool that captures the first three key principles of risk minimization. Most higher headquarters will not let training or combat missions proceed without a risk assessment that proves thought went into minimizing or eliminating risk. There are many different varieties of risk assessment cards. The example on the next page is one of the more simple cards you will find. I recommend this example for use while attending OCS.

RISK MANAGEMENT WORK SHEET

A. MISSION OR TASK	B. DATE/TIME GROUP(begin/end)	C. DATE PREPARED

D. Prepared By : (Rank, Last Name, Duty Position)

E. Task	F. Identify Hazards	G. Assess Hazards	H. Develop Controls	I. Determine Residual Risk	J. Implement Controls

K. Determine overall mission/task risk level after controls are implemented (circle one)

LOW (L) MODERATE (M) HIGH (H) EXTREMELY HIGH (E)

---FOLD---

WORK SHEET INSTRUCTIONS

BLOCK	INSTRUCTIONS
A-D	*SELF EXPLANATORY*
E	*IDENTIFY TASK RELATING TO THE MISSION OR TASK IN BLOCK A*
F	*IDENTIFY HAZARDS-* Identify hazards by reviewing METT-T factors for the mission or task. Additional factors include historical lessons learned, experience, judgement, equipment characteristics ,warnings, and environmental considerations
G	*ASSESS HAZARDS-* Assessment includes historical lessons learned, intuitive analysis, experience, judgement, equipment characteristics, warnings, and environmental considerations. Determine initial risk for each hazard by applying the Risk Assessment Matrix. Enter risk level for each hazard.
H	*DEVELOP CONTROLS-* Develop one or more controls for each hazard that will either eliminate the hazard or reduce the risk (Probability and/or Severity) of a hazardous incident. Specify Who, What, Where, Why, When, and How for each control. Enter controls.
I	*DETERMINE RESIDUAL RISK-* Determine the residual risk for each hazard by applying the Risk Assessment Matrix. Enter the residual level for each hazard.
J	*IMPLEMENT CONTROLS-*Decide how each control will be put into effect or communicated to the personnel who will make it happen (written or verbal instruction, tactical, safety, garrison SOPs, and rehearsals). Enter controls.
K	*DETERMINE OVERALL MISSION/TASK RISK-*Select the highest risk level and circle it. This will become the overall mission or task risk level. The commander decides whether the controls are sufficient to accept the level of residual risk. If the risk is too great too continue, the commander directs development of additional controls. *SUPERVISE AND EVALUATE-* This last step is not on the worksheet. Plan how each control will be monitored for implementation (continuous supervision, spot checks) and reassess hazards as the situation changes. Determine if the controls worked and if they can be improved. Pass on as Lessons Learned.

NOTE

DETAILED INFORMATION ON THE USE OF THIS WORKSHEET PLUS HOW TO DETERMINE VARIOUS LEVELS OF RISK CAN BE FOUND IN FM 100-14 CHAPTERS 2 & 3

Chapter 20

Interview with OCS Graduates and TAC Staff

"By their fruits ye shall know them."

— Matthew 7:20

I sent letters to four former OCS graduates (two Federal and two State) asking the same questions. One of these is a former TAC for OCS. The six questions cover important areas I see as potential barriers to success while attending OCS. If you read nothing else, read this section of the book and then put it back on the shelf.

* * *

Q. What is your current Army assignment?

A. B. CO 422nd ESB, XO/1st Platoon Leader, Las Vegas, Nevada

Q. What was your commissioning source? Looking back, do you feel it prepared you for being a 2LT?

A. My commissioning source was State Traditional OCS. Yes, OCS prepares you to become a more adaptive leader. You have so many curve balls coming at you that you have to learn how to have back-up plans and work around things. It teaches problem solving skills.

Q. If someone could have told you one thing prior to entering your commissioning source to make life easier, what would it have been?

A. Really read up on Drill & Ceremony and master the OPORD format. And when the tempo gets high, your adrenalin starts pumping, you got someone screaming down your throat, you have sweat running down your face, you don't know what to do, just take a second and calm down. The yelling and tempo is just a diversion to put you under pressure and see how well you react.

Q. Name a few things candidates can do to prepare themselves physically for OCS.

A. High Intensity training. It wasn't the PT sessions in the morning or even the smoke sessions through the day that wore you out. It was just the constant pace of the day-to-day. It is very fast and goes all day. Hiking, running, push-ups, sit-ups . . .

Q. What can a candidate do while at OCS to stay out of the limelight of the TAC staff?

A. Don't try and hide is the best thing, actually. If you're always in the back of formation and never stepping up then you're asking for it. Being an individual is the worst way to go through OCS. To complete all tasks required of you cannot be done without help and support from your classmates. Do not make them look bad in order to make yourself look good. The rest of your class will see this and your TACs will see this and no one will respect you for it.

Q. What do you think is the hardest part about OCS? What was the best part?

A. The hardest part of the program I did was that it was eighteen months long, but broken up into thirteen different weekends. Staying motivated to complete it was very hard. Every month getting on a plane at 0600 on Friday and not getting home until 2200-2300 on Sunday was a drain.

The best part is the memories. I met some great friends that I still talk to every month. And of course the day you finish was also right up there as the best part.

It's all worth it when you pin on the bar.

David Tallman*
2LT NVANG

* Lieutenant Tallman was one of my candidates from WAANG State Traditional OCS Class 51. He and two other candidates traveled from Nevada to Washington state each month to attend traditional OCS because Nevada lacked the bodies to put on their own State OCS. To make matters more complicated, Lieutenant Tallman tore a ligament in his knee halfway through the program and did the majority of the field problems during Phase II on a bum knee. Two years have passed and he has since had the knee operated on and is back to full strength. His personal strength and determination continue to impress me to this day.

* * *

Q. What is your current Army assignment?

A. RRC – OSM, Officer Recruiter, Camp Murray, Washington

Q. What was your commissioning source? Looking back, do you feel it prepared you for being a 2LT?

A. Federal OCS. It prepared me for the basics in military leadership but didn't fully address the many other facets of being an officer.

Q. If someone could have told you one thing prior to entering your commissioning source to make life easier, what would it have been?

A. The officer is the manager and the NCO is the supervisor. Managers walk the floor, understand all the inner workings, and are able to execute all TTPs, but DO NOT over step into the supervisors/NCO's role. Managers know their people, their families, their issues, their lives. Managers ensure the supervisors are executing. There is never a "micro" in manager, if you do your job right you don't have to do the supervisor's job.

Q. Name a few things candidates can do to prepare themselves physically for OCS.

A. Do cross-fit. If you think walking out of the gym after a good "pump" is what working out means, then you will suck wind. Do cross-fit. Plan your day to workout first thing in the morning, then eat, then go to work. That way it will prepare you for the environment you will be thrust into during training. The most basic principles of eating are carbohydrate-based. Think of it like this: Eat like a king for breakfast, a prince for lunch and a pauper for dinner. That is simply talking about carbohydrates . . . not about types of food.

Q. What can a candidate do while at OCS to stay out of the limelight of the TAC staff?

A. Study before you get there to know the material. Don't be a know it all, just execute well and show your buddies so they stay out of trouble.

Q. What do you see as the hardest part about OCS? What was the best part?

A. Not being an idiot . . .

Lucas G. Whitehall*
CPT WAANG

* Captain Whitehall works full time for Recruiting Command in Washington state. His main duty is to fill the ranks of the Washington Army National Guard with new lieutenants. He served four years on active duty that included a 16-month deployment to Iraq before joining the Washington Army National Guard. He is a terrific officer and one of those people who really grasps the concept of leadership.

* * *

Q. What is your current Army assignment?

A. 347th Company-USAR, Commanding, Farrel, Pennsylvania

Q. What was your commissioning source? Looking back, do you feel it prepared you for being a 2LT?

A. Federal OCS. I did OCS at Fort Benning from May 2004 - July 2004. I feel Fort Benning did a solid job of getting me ready for being a 2LT. However, nothing really prepares you for being an officer other than being an officer. I learned a lot at Fort Benning. . . . I learned more once I was in charge of a platoon.

Q. If someone could have told you one thing prior to entering your commissioning source to make life easier, what would it have been?

A. If you make a decision, even if it turns out to be a bad one, stick with it. It's better to decide to do something, and have it be wrong, than to sit around wondering what to do.

Q. Name a few things candidates can do to prepare themselves physically for OCS.

A. Run and jog . . . a lot. We ran every day while at Fort Benning. Get used to drinking water and Gatorade. During the first eleven weeks of OCS we were allowed to drink water, Gatorade, and milk.

Cut back on the drinking and smoking. Take some boxing or self-defense classes . . . at some point you'll be asked to go into the pit and use Army combative. Do more than just sit-ups and push-ups. We used every muscle in some way, every day.

Q. What can a candidate do while at OCS to stay out of the limelight of the TAC staff?

A. If you make a mistake, and are called on it, admit it. If you get punished for something, just accept the punishment and move on. Learn how to help out your buddies, and they'll help you out, too.

Q. What do you see as the hardest part about OCS? What was the best part?

A. While I did struggle at times, and I did wonder "what am I doing here" at times, I have to say there really wasn't anything "hardest" about going to OCS. It was a chance to really, really, REALLY, challenge myself and see what stuff I'm made of. The best part of OCS was during Senior Phase, when the Basic and Intermediate candidates had to salute us.

Mike Thomas*
CPT USAR

* Captain Thomas and I attended Officer Basic Course together in 2004-2005. He is a smart officer with a good attitude. He has one deployment under his belt and is currently a company commander of a Quartermaster unit in the Army Reserves.

* * *

Q. What is your current Army assignment?

A. A 181 BSB, Commanding, Camp Murray, Washington

Q. What was your commissioning source? Looking back, do you feel it prepared you for being a 2LT?

A. State Traditional OCS. Tennessee Military Academy, OCS. I fully believe that OCS prepared me. It certainly humbled me and taught me how to overcome obstacles.

Q. If someone could have told you one thing prior to entering your commissioning source to make life easier, what would it have been?

A. I wish someone would have told me to be an "out of the box thinker." Too often we tend to rely heavily on regulations, which don't always fit every situation we come across.

Q. Name a few things candidates can do to prepare themselves physically for OCS.

A. Go in with a positive attitude and an open mind. Be willing to move outside of your comfort zone and embrace constructive criticism. Maintain a low level of stress. These few things prepare you mentally to make you physically tough.

Q. What can a candidate do while at OCS to stay out of the limelight of the TAC staff?

A. Be a team player at all times. Don't be THAT guy who knows it all. Even if you know the answers to all the questions, have done the training a thousand times, never let the TAC know that. Shine when the TAC is not around. It will payoff in the peer evaluations, where it matters most.

Q. What do you see as the hardest part about OCS? What was the best part?

A. The hardest part was absorbing so much information at one time. OCS is an environment for the strong minded. It's challenging mentally and physically, which in turn helps to develop the candidate into a better leader. The best part was completing the program and feeling like I really accomplished something. Too often we go to a military school and everything is handed to us. NOT in OCS. You earn your commission when it's done.

Selina Riedel*
CPT WAANG

* CPT Riedel is a former TAC Officer for OCS as well as a former candidate and currently a company commander. In my experience working with her, she is a terrific officer and treats all around her with respect. She is another officer who really understands what leadership entails.

Conclusion

This book has one qualification: each specific OCS program will have OC Guides that correspond with their program. Utilize their OC guide for specifics about their program. This book provides an example of what the overall OCS experience is all about. The intent is not to replace any OCS programs specific guidance.

With that in mind, if you were on the fence about attempting OCS when you picked this book up, I hope you now have a clearer idea about what OCS entails. OCS is for soldiers who have the ability to work as part of a team, and not for those who live for individual accomplishments. No one completes OCS without depending upon classmates for support.

Thank you for making the choice to serve your country. All Americans benefit from the sacrifices the men and women of the U.S. military make voluntarily each and every day. As an officer, you represent the most professional military in history. Always put your soldiers' needs above yours and listen to your NCO corps. Make sure you recognize your family's sacrifice routinely. They may not wear the uniform, but they feel the strain of deployments and otherwise long hours of service as much as the soldier.

Good luck!

Appendix A

References

Below is information I found helpful not only in writing this book, but throughout my career. This book is organized so you can read, understand, and remember all you need to know before you to go OCS. However, I recommend you also visit these sites and read other titles in what should be a continuous quest for knowledge. Remember, officers never stop learning.

http://www.armyocs.com/

Former Federal OCS graduates do a good job posting important information about Federal OCS, including an interesting historical perspective of how and why OCS was created.

http://www.armyocsng.com/portal/index.php

The same Federal OCS graduates mentioned above created a link, much like the Federal OCS site, that has blogs for questions and answers for perspective RC candidates. You will need to generate a username and password to get to most of the pertinent information.

https://sdguard.ngb.army.mil/sites/196rti/ocsbn/default.aspx

The South Dakota Army National Guard is home to the 196th Regional Training Institute. This site has many of the required documents for candidates and TAC staff to use in support of their state program. This is the most comprehensive site you will find for state.

http://alguard.state.al.us/ocs.htm

The Alabama Army National Guard is home to the 200th RTI. This site has many of the same forms the Federal site and South Dakota site have, but are specific for Region D candidates.

http://www.army.mil/usapa/epubs/index.html

Every field manual, Army regulation or form the Army has ever created can be found here. This is the first place I go when I need a publication or a form. An Army Knowledge Online (AKO) password is necessary.

http://platoonleader.army.mil/

From lessons learned to new TTPs from the front lines, this website is an invaluable tool for company grade officers. Get on the post and read some of the information. It's almost as good as experiencing it yourself.

Appendix B

Useful Field Manuals (FMs) and Army Regulations (ARs)

FM 7-8 (now FM 3-21.8): Infantry Rifle Platoon and Squad

FM 22-5 (now FM 3-21.5): Drill and Ceremonies

FM 101-5 (now FM 5-0): Army Planning and Orders Preparation

FM 101-5-1 (now FM 1-02): Operational Terms and Graphics

FM 22-100 (now FM 6-22): Military Leadership

FM 3-24: Counterinsurgency Manual

FM 21-20: Physical Fitness Training

AR 385-10: Army Safety Program

AR 25-50: Preparing and Managing Correspondence

AR 670-1: Wear and Appearance of Army Uniforms and Insignia

AR 350-51: United States Army Officer Candidate School

Appendix C

Leadership Evaluation Report

LEADERSHIP EVALUATION REPORT

PART I - ADMINISTRATIVE DATA					
CANDIDATE NAME (Last, First MI)	LAST 4	CO/PLT/SQD	PHASE	DATE	POSITION
Snuffy Candidate J	5555	B/1/1	II	02AUG	PLATOON LEADER

RATER'S NAME / RANK / POSITION		FROM	TO
America / CPT /TAC	PERIOD COVERED	DAY 02 AUG 09 MONTH YEAR	DAY 04 AUG 09 MONTH YEAR

PART II - EXPLANATION OF RATING SYSTEM

SCALE

E (Excellent) **S** (Satisfactory) **N** (Not Satisfactory)

PART III - DUTY DESCRIPTION

Responsible for the discipline, welfare, morale, and control of all subordinates. Supervises the Platoon Sergeant and Squad Leaders in the performance of assigned tasks. Maintains the Platoon in an inspection-ready status at all times. Conducts spot inspections of individuals, platoon equipment, and platoon areas for appearance, proper care, and preparedness for training. Disseminates all necessary information to platoon members. Briefs the Platoon TAC on the status of the platoon. Maintains proper accountability of platoon at all times. Ensures that all personnel comply with regulatory guidance. Leads by example in the execution of all assigned duties according to the Candidate Guide.

PART IV - PERFORMANCE EVALUATION
(ARMY VALUES, CORE LEADER COMPETENCIES, AND LEADER ATTRIBUTES IAW FM 6-22)

ARMY VALUES	ACTS IAW		REMARKS
LOYALTY	Y	N	
DUTY	Y	N	
RESPECT	Y	N	
SELFLESS SERVICE	Y	N	
HONOR	Y	N	
INTEGRITY	Y	N	
PERSONAL COURAGE	Y	N	

Comments mandatory on a DA Form 4856 for all "NO" entries

ARNGOCS Form 1 - January 2009 Local Reproduction Authorized PAGE 1 OF 7

LEADERSHIP EVALUATION REPORT

In pages 2 thru 6 comments must be made on at least two Leads Competencies, at least two Develops Competencies, and at least one Achieves Competencies. Each evaluated competency must be complemented by at least one Attribute. See Appendix A, FM 6-22 Army Leadership.

PART IV - PERFORMANCE EVALUATION CONTINUED
Core Competencies - LEADS (must evaluate at least two Leads Competencies)

Leads Others	RATING			REMARKS
	E	S	N	
Established and imparts clear intent and purpose				
Uses appropriate influence techniques to energize others				
Conveys the significance of the work			X	ONE APFT FAILURE AND ONE BODY FAT FAILURE REFLECTS LACK OF EMPHASIS ON IMPORTANCE OF PHYSICAL FITNESS.
Maintains and enforces high professional standards				
Balances requirements of mission with welfare of followers				
Extends Influence Beyond the Chain of Command	**RATING**			**REMARKS**
	E	S	N	
Understands sphere of influence, means of influence, and limits of influence			X	DID NOT UTALIZED COC WELL PRIOR TO COMMAND INSPECTION. TIME AVAILABLE WAS NOT UTALIZED EFFECTIVLY.
Builds trust				
Negotiates for understanding, builds consensus, and resolves conflict		X		COMMUNICATED IMPORTANT INFORMATION UP AND DOWN COC EFFECTIVELY .
Builds and maintains alliances				
CANDIDATES LAST NAME	Snuffy			

ARNGOCS Form 1 - January 2009 Local Reproduction Authorized PAGE 2 OF 7

LEADERSHIP EVALUATION REPORT

PART IV - PERFORMANCE EVALUATION CONTINUED Core Competencies - LEADS (must evaluate at least two Leads Competencies)				
Leads By Example	RATING			REMARKS
	E	S	N	
Displays character by modeling the Army Values consistently through actions, attitudes, and communications				
Exemplifies the Warrior Ethos				
Demonstrates commitment to the Nation, Army, unit, Soldiers, community, and multinational partners				
Leads with confidence in adverse situations				
Demonstrates technical and tactical knowledge and skills		X		OPORD WAS CREATED AND PUT OUT TO PLATOON IN A TIMELY FASHION. OPORD WAS COMPETANT FOR A FIRST ATTEMPT.
Understands the importance of conceptual skills and models them to others				
Seeks and is open to diverse ideas and points of view				
Communicates	RATING			REMARKS
	E	S	N	
Listens actively				
Determines information-sharing strategies				
Employs engaging communication techniques				
Conveys thoughts and ideas to ensure shared understanding		X		OPORD WAS COMPLETED TO STANDARD AND ON TIME. WILL CONTINUE TO IMPROVE AS HE PROGRESSES THROUGH PROGRAM.
Presents recommendations so others understands advantages				
Is sensitive to cultural factors in communication				
CANDIDATES LAST NAME	Snuffy			

ARNGOCS Form 1 - January 2009 Local Reproduction Authorized PAGE 3 OF 7

LEADERSHIP EVALUATION REPORT

PART IV - PERFORMANCE EVALUATION CONTINUED Core Competencies - DEVELOPS (must evaluate at least two Develops Competencies)				
	RATING			REMARKS
Creates a Positive Environment	E	S	N	
Fosters teamwork, cohesion, cooperation, and loyalty				
Encourages subordinates to exercise initiative, accept responsibility, and take ownership				
Creates a learning environment				
Encourages open and candid communications				
Encourages fairness and inclusiveness				
Expresses and demonstrates care for people and their well-being			X	DECIDED TO EAT PRIOR TO HIS TROOPS DURING FIRST FEW MEALS. REFLECTS SELFISHNESS AND LACK OF SOLDIER CARE.
Sets and maintains high expectations for individuals and teams				
Accepts reasonable setbacks and failures				
	RATING			REMARKS
Prepares Self	E	S	N	
Maintains mental and physical health and well-being				
Maintains self awareness: employs self understanding and recognizes impact on others				
Evaluates and incorporates feedback from others			X	LACK OF TIME MANAGEMENT AND INCORPORATING LESSONS FROM PRIOR OCS CLASS HELPED ENSURE FAILURE DURING COMMAND INSPECTION.
Expands knowledge of technical, technological, and tactical areas				
Expands conceptual and interpersonal capabilities				
Analyzes and organizes information to create knowledge				
Maintains relevant cultural awareness				
CANDIDATES LAST NAME	Snuffy			

ARNGOCS Form 1 - January 2009 Local Reproduction Authorized PAGE 4 OF 7

LEADERSHIP EVALUATION REPORT

PART IV - PERFORMANCE EVALUATION CONTINUED Core Competencies - DEVELOPS (must evaluate at least two Develops Competencies)				
Develops Others	RATING E	S	N	REMARKS
Assesses current developmental needs of others		X		DURING SECOND COMMAND INSPECTION HELD 24 HOURS LATER, SHOWED VAST IMPROVMENT. REFLECTED ABILITY TO LEARN AND DEVELOPE OTHERS.
Fosters job development, job challenge, and job enrichment				
Counsels, coaches, and mentors				
Builds team or group skills and processes				

PART IV - PERFORMANCE EVALUATION CONTINUED Core Competencies - ACHIEVES (must evaluate at least one Achieves Competencies)				
Gets Results	RATING E	S	N	REMARKS
Prioritizes, organizes, and coordinates taskings for teams or other organizational structures/groups				
Identifies and accounts for individual and group capabilities and commitment to task				
Designates, clarifies, and deconflicts roles				
Identifies, contends for, allocates, and manages resources				
Seeks, recognizes, and takes advantages of opportunities to improve performance				
Makes feedback part of work processes				
Executes plans to accomplish the mission			X	APFT FAILURE AS A PLATOON REFLECTS LACK OF PROPER MOTIVATION. FAILED TO GET GOOD RESULTS.
Identifies and adjusts to external influences on the mission or taskings and organization				
CANDIDATES LAST NAME	Snuffy			

ARNGOCS Form 1 - January 2009 Local Reproduction Authorized PAGE 5 OF 7

LEADERSHIP EVALUATION REPORT

PART IV - PERFORMANCE EVALUATION CONTINUED
Attributes
(each of the evaluated Core Leader Competencies must be complemented with at least one Attribute)

A Leader of Character	RATING E	RATING S	RATING N	REMARKS
Army Values				
Empathy		X		REQUESTED SPECIAL PRIVLAGES FOR SOLDIER WITH UNCOMMON FAMILY ISSUES. SHOWS SOLDIER CARE.
Warrior Ethos				

A Leader with Presence	RATING E	RATING S	RATING N	REMARKS
Military bearing				
Physically fit				
Confident				
Resilient		X		TOOK COMMAND INSPECTION FAILURE IN STRIDE. IMPROVED ON RE-INSPECTION SHOWS HEART.

A Leader with Intellectual Capacity	RATING E	RATING S	RATING N	REMARKS
Agility				
Judgment				
Innovative			X	FAILED TO TAKE INITIATIVE AND DELEGATE EFFECTIVELY DURING BARRAKS INSPECTION.
Interpersonal tact				
Domain knowledge				

CANDIDATES LAST NAME	Snuffy

ARNGOCS Form 1 - January 2009 Local Reproduction Authorized PAGE 6 OF 7

LEADERSHIP EVALUATION REPORT

PART V - PERFORMANCE RECOMMENDATIONS and SUMMARY OF COUNSELING

Overall Evaluation

E (Excellent) **S** (Satisfactory) **N** (Not Satisfactory)

Summary of Counseling and Recommendations

OC SNUFFY IS NOT OPERATING AT THE LEVEL OF A PHASE II OFFICER CANDIDATE. DURING HIS TIME AS PLATOON LEADER, HE WAS RATED ON FOUR CRITICAL EVENTS.

1. OPORD CREATION- HIS PLATOON OPORD WAS OK FOR A FIRST ATTEMPT. HE UNDERSTOOD HOW THE PARAGRAPHS WERE LAID OUT AND HIS MISSION STATEMENT WAS TOO LONG. OVERALL THE OPORD WAS TOO LONG AND HAD TOO MUCH FLUF, OR UNNESSARY INFORMATION.
2. EFFECTIVELY USE COC BETWEEN DRILLS- KEPT TAC INFORMED OF ALL POTENTIAL TRAINING DISTRACTORS. ALL ISSUED WERE ADDRESSED RESULTING IN 100% ATTENDANCE DURING DRILL.
3. PLATOON APFT- ONE SOLDIER FAILED (POTENTIAL INJURY) AND ONE FAILED TAPE. OVERALL PLT AVERAGE (MINUS INJURED) IS 244, WHICH NEEDS TO BE IMPROVED.
4. BARRAKS INSPECTION- FAILED TO USED AVAILABLE TIME WISELY. 15 GIGS WERE ALLOWED, 23 WERE ASSESSED. SHOWED IMPROVMENT DURING RE-INSPECTION.

Candidate's Plan for Improvement

REFRENCE FM 101-5, CH 5, (MDMP) paying close attention to step 11. Prepare 1 page paper reflecting on why a clear and concise mission statement is important to successful mission completion.

Due NLT 122100AUG09 to CPT AMERICA at BLDG 23 TAC SHACK.

Follow-Up

Follow-up completed:____________________ Initials:________

Rater's Signature	Date Signed
Candidate's Signature	Date Signed

ARNGOCS Form 1 - January 2009 Local Reproduction Authorized PAGE 7 OF 7

Appendix D

Recommendation for OCS Example

DEPARTMENT OF THE ARMY
___ SUPPORT GROUP
APO AE XXXXX

OFFICE SYMBOL
August 2009

MEMORANDUM FOR President, Officer Candidate Selection Board

SUBJECT: Letter of Recommendation for Officer Candidate School

1. Sergeant _________ is an outstanding Noncommissioned Officer and an exceptional leader. I consider it an honor to recommend such a fine soldier for this selection board. He has gained the respect of his peers and superiors alike.

2. Few soldiers obtain the technical and tactical proficiency he has displayed. Sergeant ______ is one of the finest soldiers within my command and he will no doubt make an excellent officer capable of leading our soldiers forward regardless of the situation. I strongly recommend that you select Sergeant _______ for Officer Candidate School. Challenge him and watch him motivate his soldiers to excel.

3. It Shall Be Done!

____
CPT, IN
Commanding

Appendix E

Officer Candidate Biography Example

One of your first assignments as an OCS student is to write an autobiography focusing on that part of your life that led you to consider becoming an Army Officer. Here are some suggestions for how to proceed with this assignment:

1. Present vital statistics: date, place of birth, places of residence, schools attended, family background, and prior military service or experiences.

2. Describe special events in your life; relate circumstances and happenings that make you who and what you are, and events you expect readers will find memorable.

3. Explain what you will contribute to society after gaining an OCS education and what you will contribute after completing OCS requirements and gaining a commission.

NOTE: One of your principal writing tasks is to develop a fluid, readable narrative of your life, so do not simply list responses to these suggested questions. Instead, weave your responses into a narrative story of your life, your expectations in life, and how this relates to your goal of earning a commission in the U.S. military.

4. Format: Your final paper will be typed or computer-printed on one side only. Number each page (except the first page-cover sheet) on the center bottom. The cover sheet format is provided. Your autobiography will start on the second page and be numbered “1” in the numbering sequence of all the remaining pages.

5. Fasten a head and shoulders photo of yourself (3" x 5" or 4" x 6" photos or digital camera printouts on high-quality paper are acceptable) in uniform (ACUs) to the bottom of the cover sheet. Use scotch tape to fasten the photo to cover sheet. Local policy/SOP may require your class to schedule a date for all of you to take photos together, or you may wish to get together with classmates and take each other's picture.

6. Evaluation: OCS staff members will evaluate your autobiography. The OCS Selection Board of Officers will read and review your autobiography to formulate initial opinions about you. Your autobiography will be judged on four criteria: content, organization, readability, and presentation. Evaluators will consider the following questions as they make their evaluation:

A. Substance: How much specific detail have you used? (Generally, the more detail the better.) How appropriate is the detail? How well does the reader get to "know" you, based solely upon your brief autobiography?

B. Organization: Does your paper develop smoothly? Does each part relate well with the rest of your paper? Do you relate your earlier life to your present situation in college? Do your expectations regarding the future emerge clearly from what you reveal of your past and present?

C. Style: Are your transitions smooth and effective? Is your writing direct and clear? Is your vocabulary familiar and unpretentious? Do you avoid long, cumbersome sentences? Is your punctuation correct? Is your document spell-checked? Overall, does your work observe the conventions of standard written English?

Below is how the front page of your autobiography will look:

OCS Student Autobiography

By

Last, First, Middle

OCS Program (state)

OCS Class Number

Date Prepared

candidate photo

Appendix F

Reports

1. 9—Line MEDEVAC REPORT

Line 1: Location of the pick-up site.

Line 2: Radio frequency, call sign, and suffix.

Line 3: Number of patients by precedence:

A: Urgent
B: Urgent Surgical
C: Priority
D: Routine
E: Convenience

Line 4: Special equipment required:

A: None
B: Hoist
C: Extraction equipment
D: Ventilator

Line 5: Number of patients:

A: Litter
B: Ambulatory

Line 6: Security at pick-up site:

N: No enemy troops in area
P: Possible enemy troops in area (approach with caution)
E: Enemy troops in area (approach with caution)
X: Enemy troops in area (armed escort required)

(* in peacetime, include number and types of wounds, injuries, and illnesses)

Line 7: Method of marking pick-up site:

A: Panels
B: Pyrotechnic signal
C: Smoke signal
D: None
E: Other

Line 8: Patient nationality and status:

A: US Military
B: US Civilian
C: Non-US Military
D: Non-US Civilian
E: EPW

Line 9: NBC Contamination:

N: Nuclear
B: Biological
C: Chemical

(* in peacetime, include number and types of wounds, injuries, and illnesses)

2. CALL FOR FIRE

"________ THIS IS ________ FIRE FOR EFFECT (OR ADJUST FIRE), OVER."

"GRID ________, DIRECTION ________ (IN MILES), OVER."

"(TARGET DESCRIPTION), OVER."

"(MUNITION REQUESTED, I.E., HIGH EXPLOSIVE, SMOKE, ETC., IN EFFECT, OVER."

(IF ADJUST FIRE): "ADD/DROP, OVER."

(IF ADJUST FIRE): "FIRE FOR EFFECT, OVER."

"END OF MISSION, (TARGET DISPOSITION, ESTIMATED CASUALTIES, ETC.), OVER."

3. SALUTE REPORT

S	
A	
L	
U	
T	
E	

4. GOTWA

G	
O	
T	
W	
A	

Appendix G

Operational Graphics and Terrain Model Kit

This appendix is to help you through the squad and field training exercise (STX, FTX) you will conduct as an Officer Candidate. Operational terms and graphics will be used at OCS and throughout the rest of your career, so this appendix is designed to help introduce you to many of these terms and concepts. While I only include the basics hat company grade officers will consistently deal with, this will provide familiarization to new 2LTs.

The terrain model symbols and graphics are intended to be cut out of the book, laminated and used in your terrain model kit. While there are more colorful and robust terrain model kits available on the market, this will provide an Officer Candidate with ample graphics for an STX/FTX lane sand table.

Basic Symbols

Friendly Unit

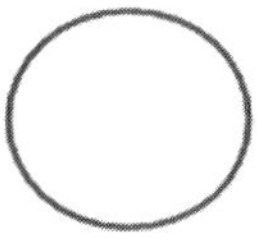

Installation
or
Friendly Air/Sea

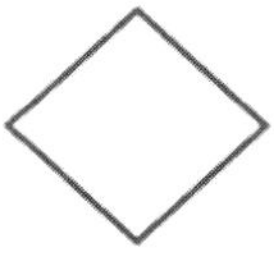

Enemy Unit

Modifiers

Size Indicators

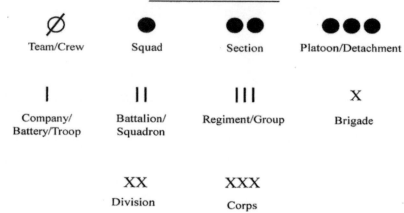

Ø	●	●●	●●●
Team/Crew	Squad	Section	Platoon/Detachment
I	II	III	X
Company/ Battery/Troop	Battalion/ Squadron	Regiment/Group	Brigade
	XX	XXX	
	Division	Corps	

Modifiers

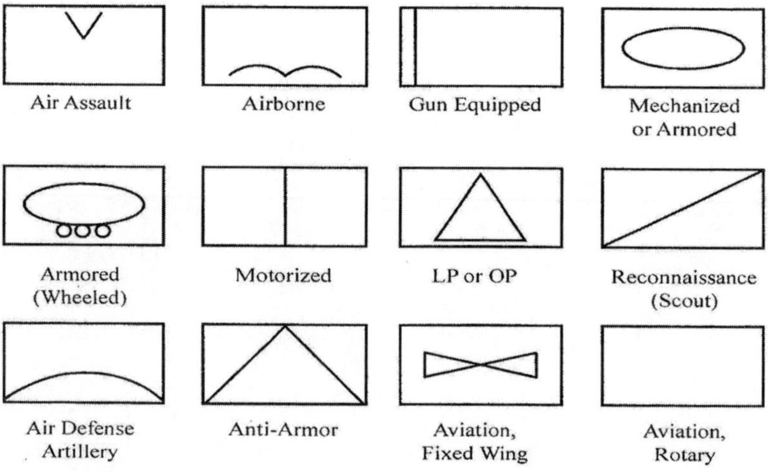

Modifiers

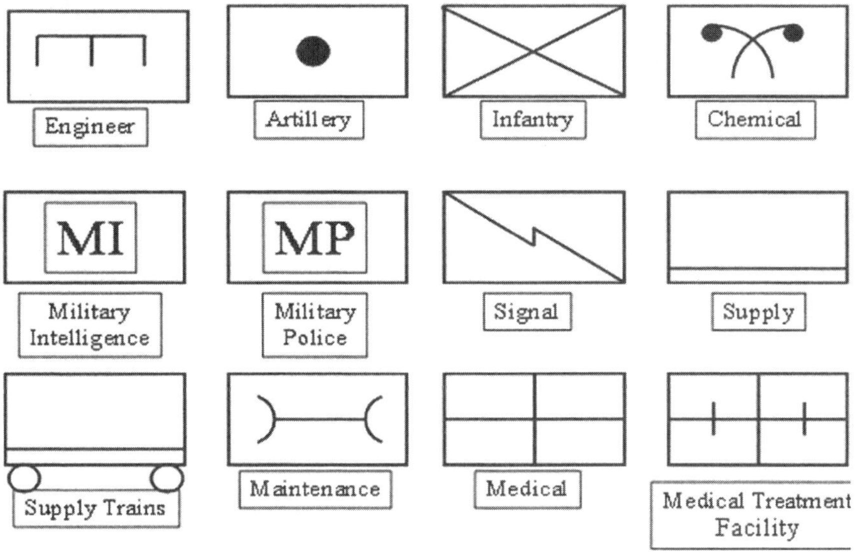

Operational Graphics

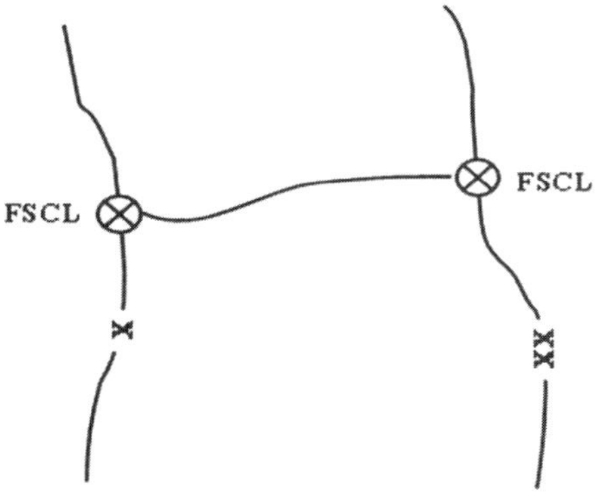

Sample

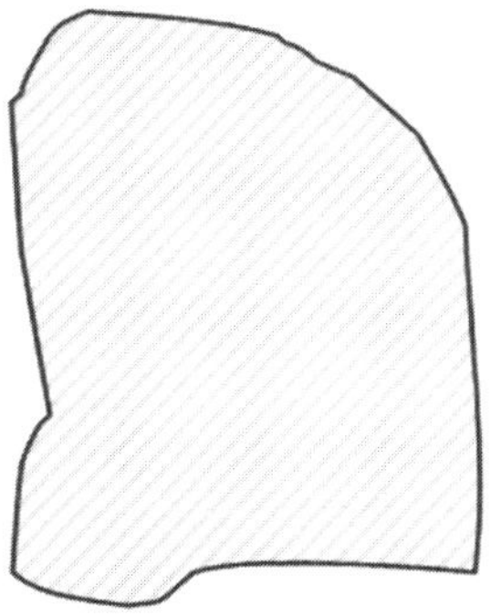

Contaminated Area, NBC

Operational Graphics

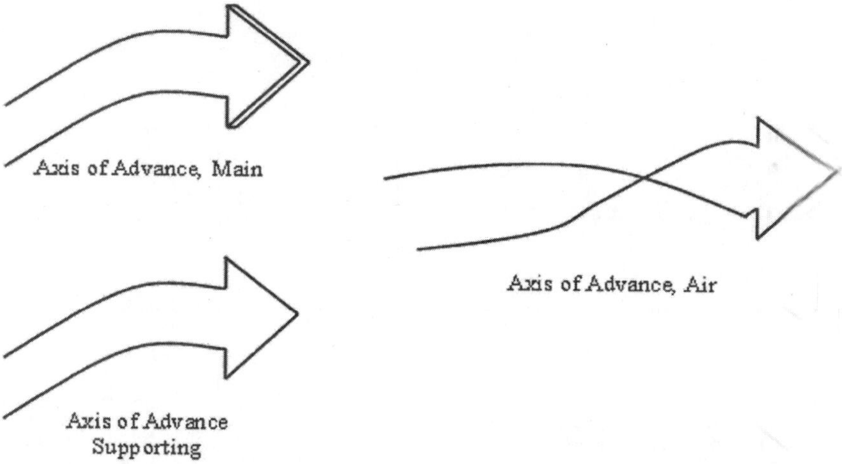

Operational Graphics

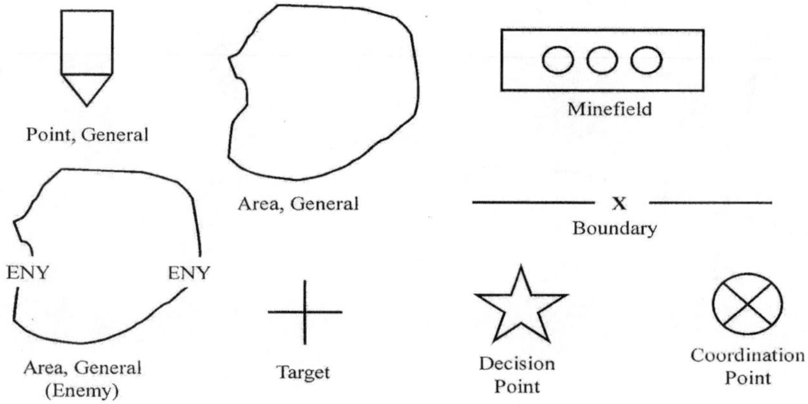

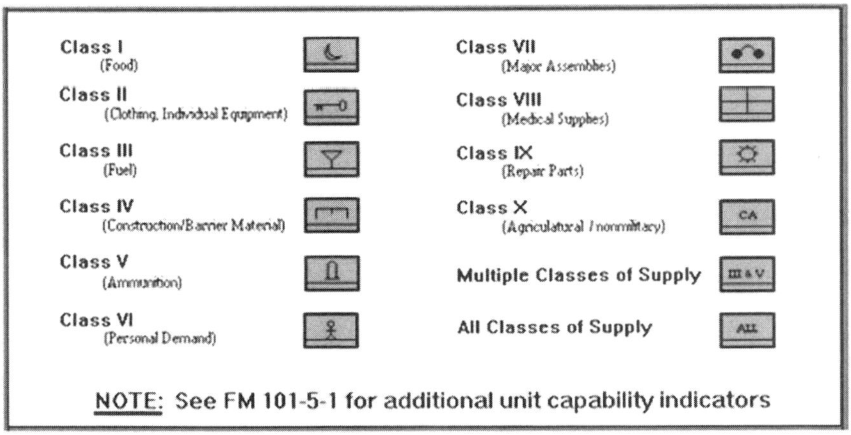
Class I
(Food)
Class II
(Clothing, Individual Equipment)
Class III
(Fuel)
Class IV
(Construction/Barrier Material)
Class V
(Ammunition)
Class VI
(Personal Demand)
Class VII
(Major Assemblies)
Class VIII
(Medical Supplies)
Class IX
(Repair Parts)
Class X
(Agriculatural / nonmilitary)
CA
Multiple Classes of Supply
III & V
All Classes of Supply
ALL
NOTE: See FM 101-5-1 for additional unit capability indicators

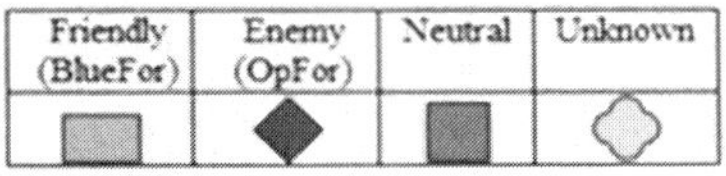
Friendly (BlueFor)
Enemy (OpFor)
Neutral
Unknown

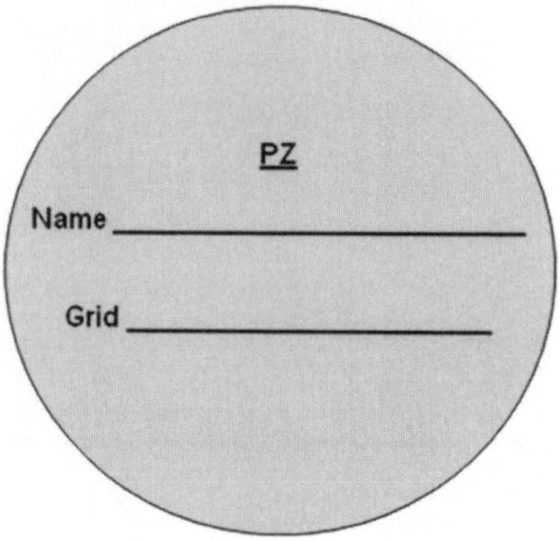
PZ
Name
Grid

CURRENT PATROL BASE
Grid

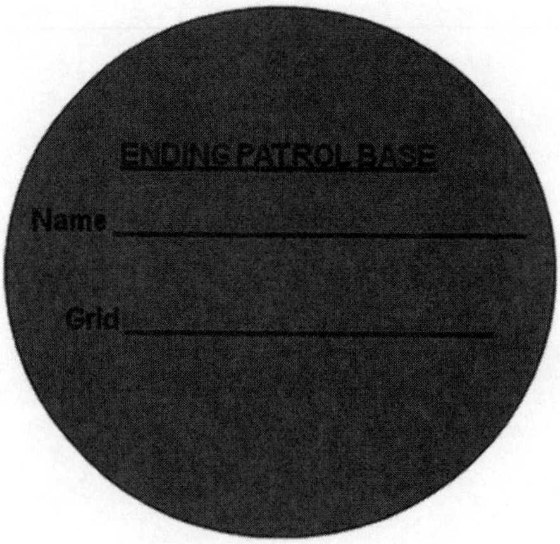
ENDING PATROL BASE
Name
Grid

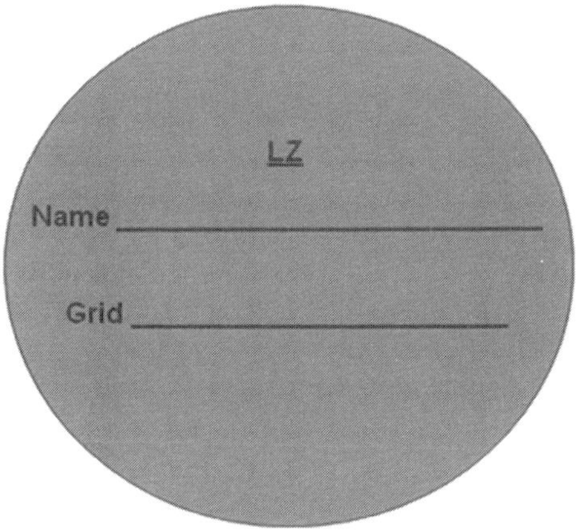
LZ
Name
Grid

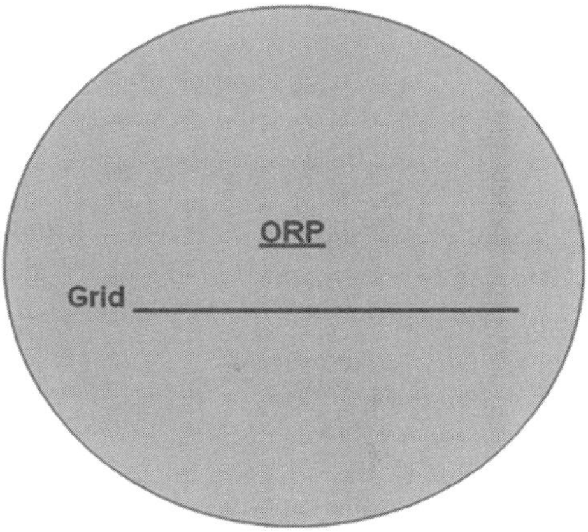
ORP
Grid

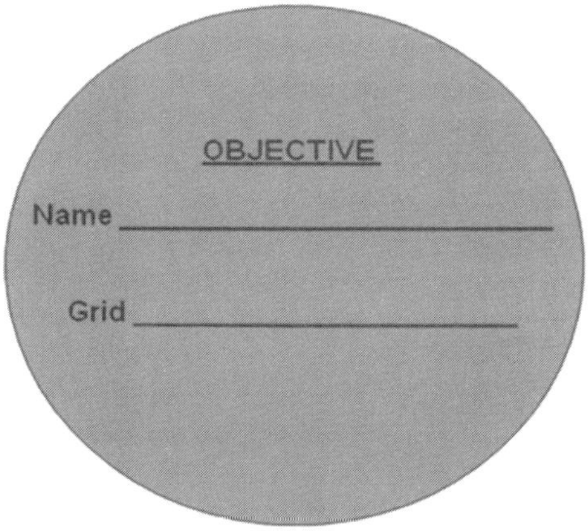
OBJECTIVE
Name
Grid

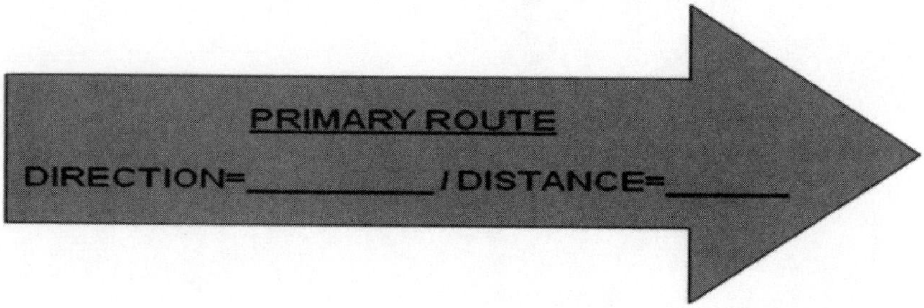
PRIMARY ROUTE
DIRECTION=__________/ DISTANCE=_______

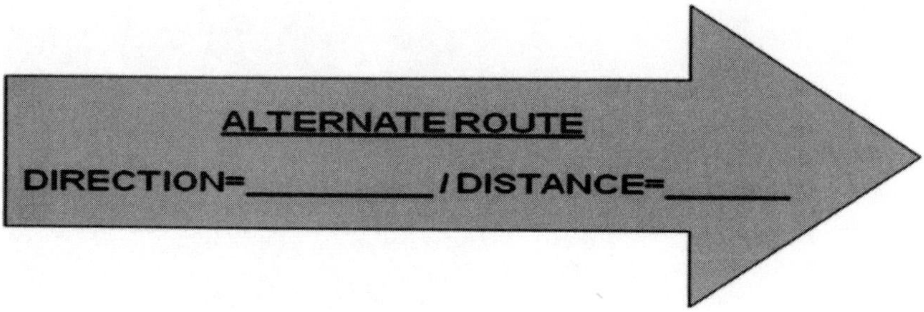
ALTERNATE ROUTE
DIRECTION=__________/ DISTANCE=_______

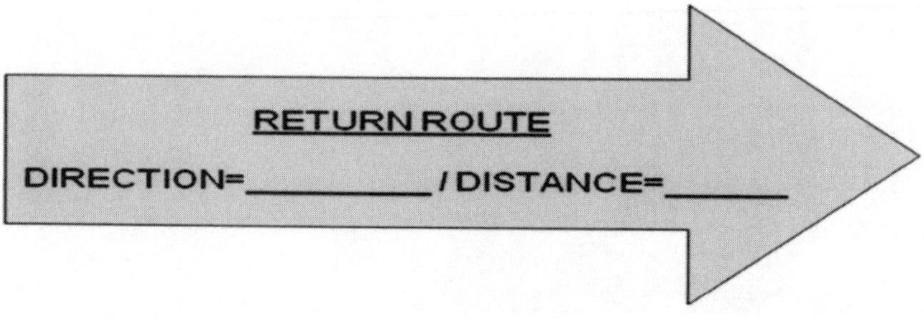
RETURN ROUTE
DIRECTION=__________/ DISTANCE=_______

A TEAM

A TEAM

2nd Squad

B TEAM

B TEAM

2nd Squad

1st Squad

1st Squad

SECURITY

SECURITY

SECURITY

DIR: __________ °

DIS: __________ m

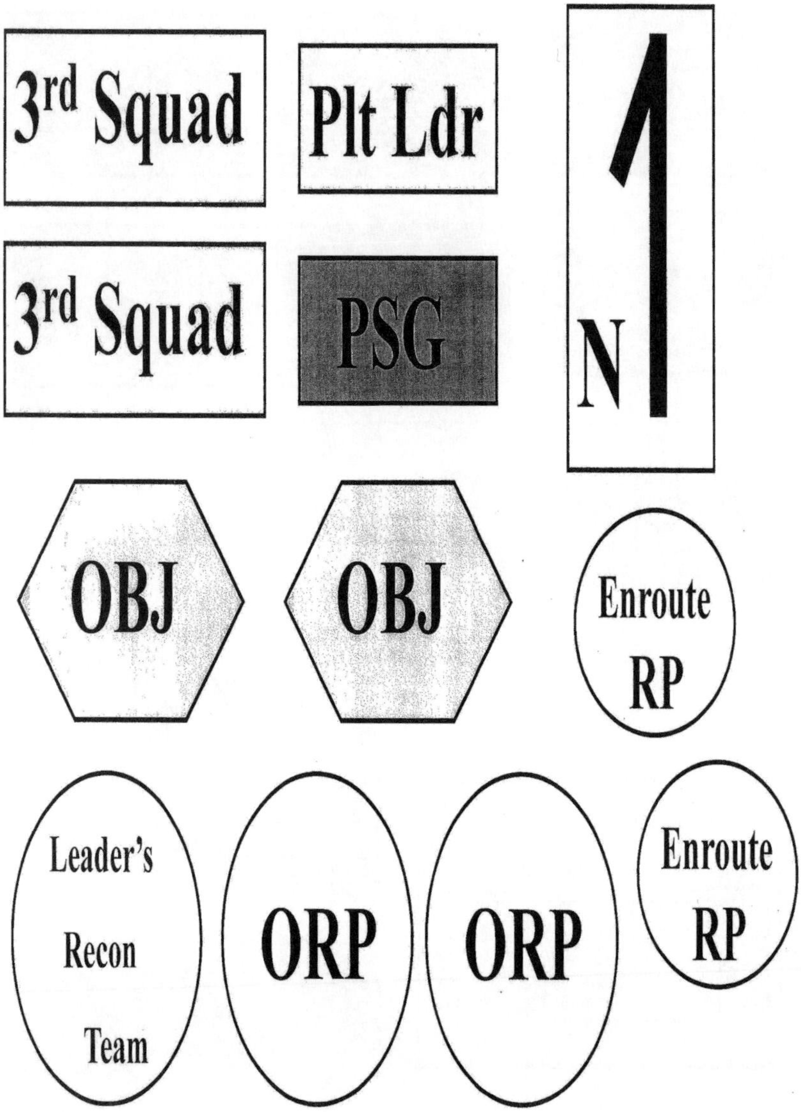
3rd Squad
Plt Ldr
N
3rd Squad
PSG
OBJ
OBJ
Enroute RP
Leader's Recon Team
ORP
ORP
Enroute RP

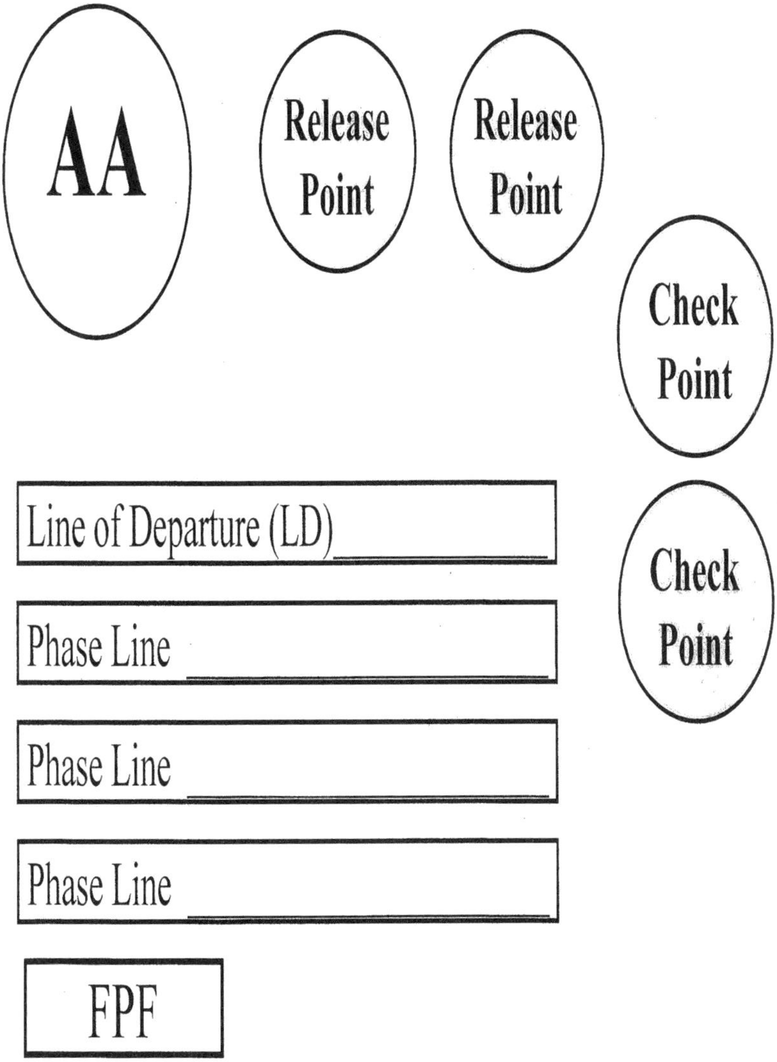
AA
Release Point
Release Point
Check Point
Check Point
Line of Departure (LD)
Phase Line
Phase Line
Phase Line
FPF

Sqd Ldr

LOA

PB

PB

LOA

BUNKER CLEARING

LISTENING HALT

DIR: ____________________

DIS: ____________________ m

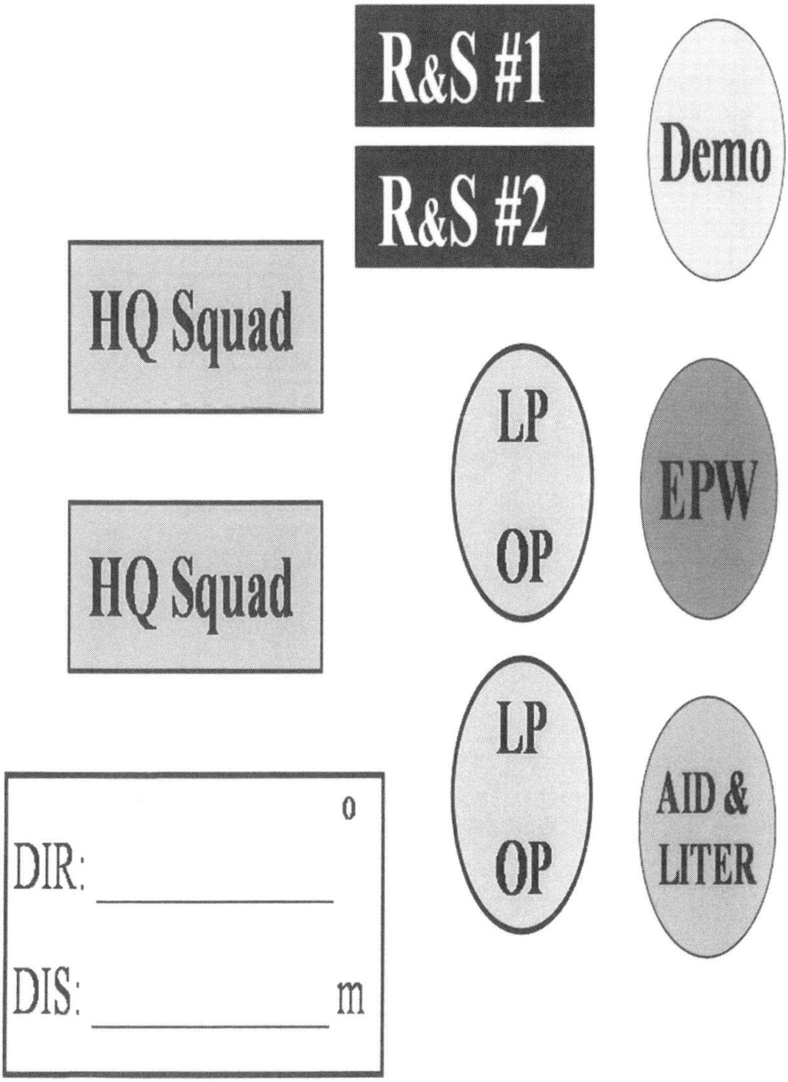
R&S #1
R&S #2
Demo
HQ Squad
LP
OP
EPW
HQ Squad
LP
OP
AID &
LITER
DIR: °
DIS: m

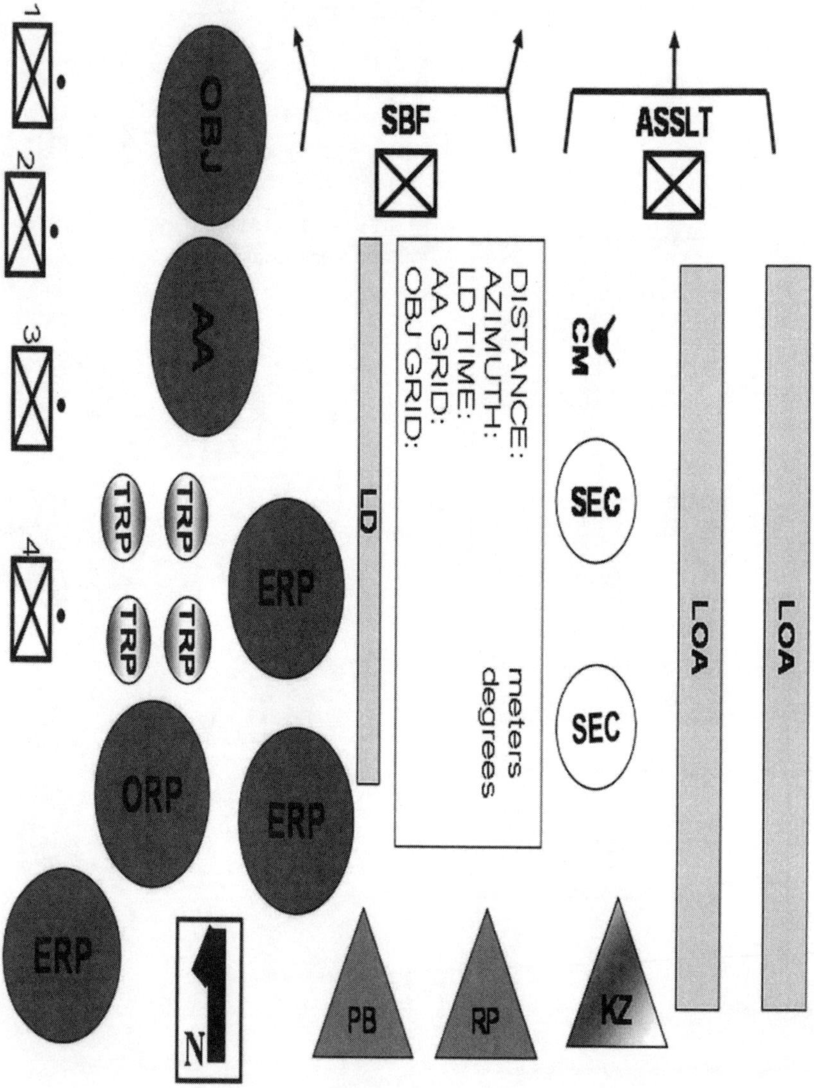
1
2
3
4
OBJ
AA
SBF
ASSLT
LD
DISTANCE: meters
AZIMUTH: degrees
LD TIME:
AA GRID:
OBJ GRID:
CM
SEC
SEC
LOA
LOA
TRP
TRP
TRP
TRP
ERP
ERP
ERP
ORP
N
PB
RP
KZ

Index

3/

About the Author

Ryan Pierce is a captain in the Washington Army National Guard and a 2004 graduate of the Alabama Military Academy OCS course. To date, he has served one tour in Iraq and worked three years as a TAC officer for the state OCS program in support of the Washington Army National Guard. Captain Pierce is currently serving as Commander of the 792nd Chemical Recon Company in Grandview, Washington. He holds an MBA with an emphasis in Change Leadership from City University of Seattle. He resides in Burien, Washington, with his wife of five years, Megan, and their son Bennett.